WARNING!

THE FOLLOWING IS A COLLECTION OF TRUE STORIES, OPINIONATED EDITORIALS, AND THE THOUGHTS OF A GAMER-BRO WHOSE OBSESSIONS INCLUDE CHASING WOMEN, STUFFING HIS FACE WITH FAST FOOD, AND GETTING INTO DISPUTES ON THE INTERNET OVER VIDEO GAMES. THE THINGS HE SAYS ARE OFTEN TIMES VERY CONTROVERSIAL, VERY FILTHY, AND VERY WRONG. THIS BOOK IS MEANT FOR ENTERTAINMENT PURPOSES ONLY. KRIS KAIL IS A COMEDIAN, NOT THE MESSIAH, SO DON'T TRY TO IMITATE THE THINGS HE DID.

DUDE GURLZ

Presents...

KRIS KAIL IS EXCEPTIONAL. WELL, EXCEPTIONAL IN THE SENSE THAT HE IS ATYPICAL. I MEAN HE'S A BIT OFF. HAVE YOU READ HIS FIRST BOOK? THE DUDE POOPED AND HAD THE EUREKA MOMENT TO THINK THAT THE POOP WOULD LOOK BETTER WITH HIS FALLEN SEED ON IT. AND THEN HE LEFT IT THERE FOR THE WORLD TO BEHOLD. READ THOSE SENTENCES AGAIN ONE TIME. DON'T WORRY, I'LL WAIT. ALRIGHT. SEE? HE'S EXCEPTIONAL.

THAT SAID, HE'S ONE OF THE PEOPLE I'VE MET IN THIS LIFETIME THAT I'D NEVER WANT TO HAVE LIVED WITHOUT. HE'S FUNNY, BIZAARELY CHARMING, AND SO FAR OUT OF THE STEREOTYPICAL NORM THAT HE MAKES A GUY LIKE ME FEEL BOILER PLATE. THE WORLD NEEDS MORE PEOPLE LIKE KRIS KAIL, AND MORE BOOKS LIKE HIS. NOT TO SERVE AS A MANUAL FOR HOW TO LIVE YOUR LIFE, OR HOW NOT TO, BUT TO REMIND US OF THE POSSIBILITY OF HUMAN EXCELLENCE.

ALSO, PLEASE GIVE THIS BOOK A FIVE STAR REVIEW, AND BUY THE SURE TO BE BAN'D BOOK, AVAILABLE AT WWW.SURETOBEBANNED.COM

-TRUNKS
Sure to be BAND

SLACKER'S INFERNO
THE TRIALS AND HARDSHIPS OF A
SLACKER'S QUEST FOR GURLZ, LUNCH, AND MONEY

BY KRIS KAIL

2

TABLE OF CONTENTS

4

PROLOGUE

"You better back up, Doc! You don't have enough road to get the DeLorean up to 88 miles per hour!" said young Martin McFly anxiously as he watched the crazy look in the Doc's eyes.

"Roads? Where we're going, we don't need roads." Replied the Doc, who obviously knew what he was doing and thought that Marty should just shut the fuck up and relax.

That's how my favorite sequel of all time, *Back to the Future Part II*, began. It was quite possibly one of the greatest and best sequels of all time to one of the greatest and best films of all time. *Back to the Future* will forever be remembered as the movie that successfully made light of taboo topics such as incest, date rape, and the unbreakable bond between an old man and a young boy. The sequel realized the first one was a tad silly with all that, so they did away with it and instead of there being an incestuous relationship between mother and son, the mother married her rapist and the rapist attempted to kill his step-son by holding him at gun point on the roof of the casino he owned. I remember watching these movies as a young lad and laughing 'till the cows came home.

But what does this mean? What does this mean to you, the reader, who unknowingly paid an exorbitant amount of money to hold this crappy book in their hands? Well, frankly speaking this book is a sequel. The book you hold in your hands is Part II of the *Slacker's* trilogy, of which I don't think there will be a third one. So it's a duology? Is that a word? Shut up. Anyhoo, how do you do a sequel to a book as great as *Slacker's Paradise – The Collective Writings of an Internet Radio Host*? The same way you do anything, stupid! Wait till someone hands you a bunch of cash and then just slam your fingers on the keyboard and hope what comes out of the other end isn't absolute shit.

I can name many movies and video games where the sequels were better than the originals. *Batman Returns* immediately comes to mind, as does *The Dark Knight*, and while we're on the subject of sequels, *Arkham City* was a lot better than the original. But what about sequels that stunk to high heaven? *The Godfather III*, *Rugrats Go Wild!*, *Return of the Jedi*, these are all movies that blew the big one, and guess what? They were the THIRD CHAPTER in a series of otherwise great flicks. I don't need to tell you guys that the third chapter in a series usually stinks, but the second one is usually the one that's great. That's why we're here!

Let me tell you a little about illusions, if you'll recall Chris Nolan's 2006 classic film *The Prestige*, which surprisingly for a Nolan film, had very little Batman, there are three parts to an act. The Pledge, The Turn and The Prestige. The Pledge takes something ordinary, something you already know quite well, could be an object, a person, anything you already know, and shows it to you. The Turn is when the magician takes that something ordinary and makes it do something extraordinary, you following? Then the magician takes that extraordinary something and turns it completely on its head so now it's the most amazing spectacle you've ever seen, and there you have it, The Prestige. That's what I'll be doing throughout the pages of this book.

The Pledge is the first book, the one you hopefully read before you picked this one up. If not, I'll bring you up to speed. The first book,

Slacker's Paradise, was about me finding myself as a comedian and telling my story to the world. I used stories from my own life in an effort to make the reader laugh, and I made comments about the writings I included, and kept things real and swaggy. It was a collection of things I had done up to that point, and it was me as I'd have you all know me. It was the ordinary.

What follows, though, is anything but. This is The Turn. I will take what you read in the first book and turn it on its side before your very eyes. How can I do that, you may be wondering? Well, the first book concentrated entirely on laughs. In fact, that's why I wrote it. I wanted to make the reader laugh with my crazy stories. This book will do something very different that I'm not entirely used to doing, though. I'll be showing a more human side of my character, which I only barely alluded to in the epilogue of the last book. There will still be laughs, but this time those laughs will be backed with the weight of something very real.

But what about The Prestige? Well now, I can't reveal my whole act to you before it's even performed, can I?

The reason why this book is titled *Slacker's Inferno – The Trials and Hardships of a Slacker's Quest for Gurlz, Lunch, and Money* is because I'm going to take you on a little trip back in time. Imagine, if you will, that I am the Ghost of Christmas Past and I'm taking you back to my childhood to show you how I was before I became a huge dick, and then you go "Alright this time travel thing is neat and all, but why the Hell are you showing me your past? I can't prevent anything you do, why did you bring me along in the first place?" To which I'd respond "What the heck, bro? You should be honored I decided to take you on this chill ass road trip. Jeez, show a little gratitude, it's not every day that you get to go back to the 1990's to see what life was like for a young boy." And then we ditch the memories and go get a taco because it's 1997 and Taco Bell is giving out sweet Nintendo 64 toys.

See, kids, back then we didn't have Fourth Meal, so if we wanted Taco Bell we had to substitute it for one of the other three meals throughout the day. They were never open before 11, so forget breakfast. This leaves two meals for which we could get our soft tacos. It was a disaster, they were on the brink of bankruptcy *[citation needed]*, and very few people were able to enjoy the sweet promotions they had like the chill Godzilla cups for the Matthew Broderick movie. There was just not enough time in the day! So the eggheads at Taco Bell's Research and Development Department added more time in the day. They created a fourth meal, and being the geniuses that they were, they aptly named it Fourth Meal, and it was chill. So chill that any bro that was up past 11 could mosey on down to Taco Bell and enjoy some Fourth Meal. They had saved not only the company, but the lives of many insomniacs, vampires, and prostitutes.

Anyhoo, contained in the following pages are the words that comprise the sequel to the 2011 hit book *Slacker's Paradise – The Collective Writings of an Internet Radio Host*. The sequel drops the radio host moniker as I have not hosted a radio program on the internet since that book was published. Instead, we focus more on Kristen Kail and his struggle to find himself, through fluffing his ego about childhood, his teenage years, and adulthood. And he fluffs his ego further by referring to himself in the third person.

I hope you enjoy this book more than you enjoyed the last one, and if you didn't read the last one, well, get to it. You don't need to know what happened in book one to understand book two, but it helps.

CHAPTER 1

HOW I SURVIVED MY EX-GIRLFRIEND

THE BEGINNING OF THE END

When I wrote the blog posts that are now featured in my first book Slacker's Paradise I focused on playing them up to make the reader laugh. The stories contained in that book, were 100% real, but were told in a way that would come off as hilarious. I did that purposely because I'm a comedian. That's my job. But people have asked me so many questions about those stories that I couldn't help but chronicle them all for you in true chronological order, from my humble beginning to the present day. The start of this story doesn't begin when I first started doing comedy, though. It instead starts back in 2010 when I started dating the girl I thought was the love of my life.

In June of 2010 I met Felicia, a girl who could only be described as a mix between punk-rock and Brooklyn hipster. She had short, brown hair with the side shaved like Skrillex, glasses, and she was covered in tattoos and piercings. At the time I was still living at home with my parents, and I was coasting along at a full-time job that I hated working as a security guard. I was desperately trying to avoid my job, and at the time I was writing what I thought was my ticket out of that job – the script to Destroy

All Slackers, a movie that never happened. When me and Felicia met I thought it was love at first sight, especially because on our third date we'd showed each other our emotional wounds and realized we had a lot in common.

We had spent every day of the summer together, and when she went away for a week to look at colleges and couldn't text or go online we would write letters to give to each other when she came back. It was absolutely wonderful, we were this cute little romantic couple who everyone saw and was happy for. I was so blinded by what I perceived to be happiness that I couldn't see what was actually happening.

At that time I was very hesitant to have sex, I've always been the kind to wanna wait on something like that. She would always push for it during the first couple of weeks we started dating. I didn't plan on waiting too long, but I didn't want to do it right away. Eventually I caved and we did it and it was horrible, I had a panic attack, and for like a week I just felt really shitty. It wasn't the first time I had sex, but unfortunately it was the first time I had consented to it. A few months before, I went out on a date with a girl (who was twice my size I should mention, I'm not being mean it just pertains to the story), and we had been drinking. She wanted to have sex, but I told her I didn't really want to and she pushed for it and got on top and started making out with me and just kind of pushed me to it. Since she was twice my size, pushing her off was not an option. This kind of made it difficult for me to want to actually have sex with Felicia, but I of course, caved, due to fear of her leaving me for someone better than me at everything.

As we kept going, she would always mention how she missed dating this 40 year old dude she dated before she met me. She told me it was exciting being with him, and I got really upset and said "What? I'm not exciting enough for you?" To which she responded by saying I was what she needed, and that she enjoyed being with me, but no I wasn't that exciting. I let it go, but that bothered me for a while. For the entirety of our relationship she would constantly put me down every chance she got. I felt that the reason she was doing this was because she was unhappy with me, so every day I'd take her out and spend money on her, buy her shit, pay for dinners, shit like that. I even bought her a Super Nintendo and all the games she told me she loved as a kid. What did she give me? A whole lotta nothing. In fact, one time I took her on a weekend trip down the shore and paid for everything because she didn't have any money, and when she got paid the next week from her job she blew her whole check on a tattoo.

Near the end of the summer Felicia went off to college in Long Island and for the first few weeks I'd drive there to visit her frequently, paying the $28 in combined tolls every time. After a while she started getting tired of my not being able to be at her every beck and call, and she had found someone else. So she dumped me. The dude she found was exactly what she'd always wanted me to be: covered in tattoos and piercings, fan of Blink 182 and Sum 41 and all that shit, and above all else, he was exciting.

When I say that I was devastated, that's a fucking understatement. Every day I was in constant physical and emotional pain. It got to the point where I thought pulling off a crazy 80's teen movie scheme would win her back. I went out, bought her some flowers, and drove all the way to Long Island and blasted her favorite song out of my car's speakers to get her to take me back. Guess what, it didn't work. She kind of hated me for it and thought I was a jackass. I had to face the facts, it was over. It wasn't until months later that I would realize she was a terrible girlfriend anyways.

The main thing that got me, though, was that I had given up my comedy career that summer to spend time with her. Before I met her, I was focused on actually making Destroy All Slackers into a full length animated feature film, but when we got together I had sort of lost interest. Not to mention, she hated my comedy with a PASSION. She hated my dirty jokes, my offensive humor, she hated that I was on Twitter, she hated seeing my jokes on Facebook, everything. So I stopped. I gave up comedy for her, and when she left me I didn't have a way to get it back. It was gone. I honestly contemplated suicide for a brief moment like I was a sophomore in high school again, but then I realized that tragedy makes for the best comedy. So I got back to work…

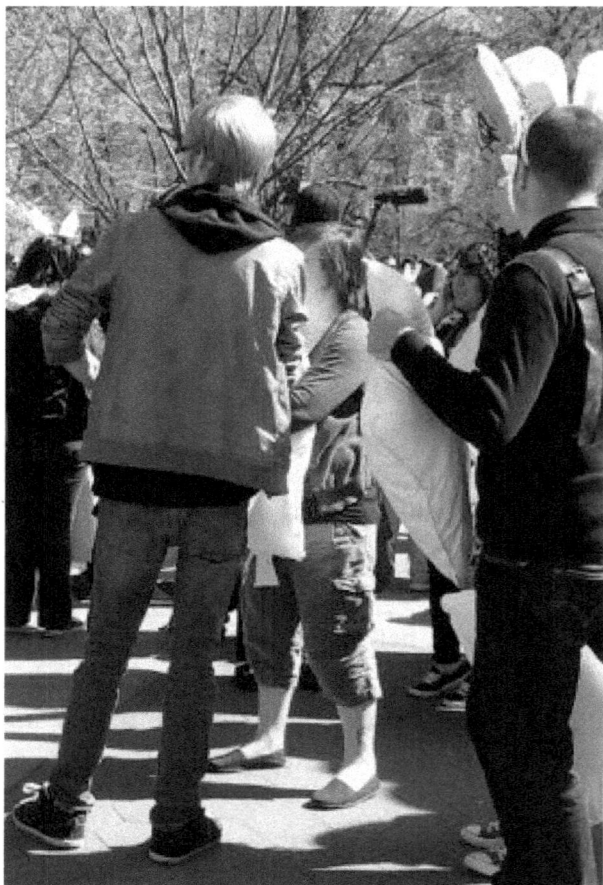

This candid photo of Felicia was taken by a friend of mine who ran into her at a flash mob pillow fight in New York City. Felicia gave her a dirty look, which prompted her to beat her senseless with her pillow. She texted me this picture while I was taking a dump to verify whether or not it was her.

"text her that picture and say 'cool hair i like ur cargo pockets'"
-lulinternet in response to me tweeting about her.

OVERCOMING TRAGEDY THROUGH COMEDY

After Felicia dumped me I was left without anything to keep me going. My job sucked, my friends were all busy, and I was broke from spending all my money on her when we were dating. My life SUCKED. Even now, I can look back and say that while the constant blubbering was excessive, my life still didn't look too enjoyable. I needed something to brighten my day up, and another girl wasn't the thing.

So I got back to work on my comedy, but I didn't start where I left off. I flat left Destroy All Slackers. The script I was so proud of, I tossed it aside for a girl like it was nothing, I didn't deserve to work on it again. Instead, I started working on stand up, and boy did I stink! I worked on an album of stand-up comedy bits called Devil May Kail that had a funny enough concept – I would recite these extremely offensive and over the top bits about topics I found amusing over 1960's production music. I wasn't confident enough in my abilities as a comic to perform it live, so I took to the internet. This was when I first REALLY started using Twitter. I would come up with humorous jokes and tweet them from my phone. I felt pretty good, good enough that I would go on my friend Juliana's college radio show The Oven, which was broadcast on Montclair State University's station 90.3 WMSC. She invited me on, I talked about my history as a comic musician, and I performed some of my bits with the accompanying music. It was a hit!

Later on, in September 2010, my buddy Dazz from The Spriter's Resource came down to New Jersey from England with his girlfriend Charlie. I tell this story all the time, they came down, I showed them New York City, we had fun, but it's an important piece of the puzzle. Nothing helps get an ex-girlfriend off your mind like good friends, and these two were loads of fun. Dazz, Charlie, Webking Pete, and myself all went to dinner every night, we checked out the different sights in New York, and we went out to a pool hall where we played pool with the dudes from the ad agency that worked with Spriter's Resource and I did some networking. This networking gave me the confidence I needed to keep going with the comedy.

One night we decided to go to Chili's for dinner, and my friend Andrew Teller wanted to come and meet Dazz because he was a HUGE fan of The Spriter's Resource. So I went and picked him up, and on the way to meet up with Dazz, Charlie, and Pete at Chili's we began having an in-depth conversation about Sonic Adventure 2. It was during this conversation that we realized we had great chemistry with each other and we'd be great as a podcast duo. Teller was the one who had the initial idea to do it, and I said why the fuck not, though it would be months before we actually decided to get to it.

Dazz and Charlie's stay wasn't long, but it was just the boost I needed to keep myself going strong. After they left I had started briefly reporting as a journalist for a gaming website, something I rarely talk about as I was a lazy asshole working for them. I was mostly a lazy asshole because 1.) their website stunk to high heaven and didn't work on ANYONE's computers, and 2.) I wasn't getting paid. It was during this time, though, that I was sent to the New York Comic Con to report on upcoming shit.

NYCC is always great fun, but it really sucks when you're there to do work and not just hang out. I ran around interviewing tons of people, got to meet Brentalfloss, and I started thinking about how I was going to get my comedy going. I needed a new website to show off my stuff, but I also figured people would be more interested in something interactive. A standard Kris Kail website wouldn't do, I needed to have a bunch of people showing off a bunch of things. This is where the idea of MUSCLETOWER first came about. We originally started it to show off a variety of things from art, to music, to comics, to podcasts, to whatever.

Things are starting to look up for me now at this point because I'd found some purpose in my life again, but we're not completely out of the clear yet. Every day I still get that same burning feeling in my gut, the rage that I felt because someone could just toss me aside like I was nothing. It was tough to move on, but I kept going.

What I thought I needed, though, was a new girlfriend…

Dazz, me, and Teller when we went out bowling. I was awesome, as usual.

THE DATING GAME

With comedy I had a reason to keep the train moving, I'm not gonna be that asshole who says comedy saved my life, but I am gonna be the asshole who says comedy gave me something to do. When you're working a shitty job that you enjoy doing for what it is but it's not exactly fulfilling, you need something to help get you through the day. Comedy was good for that, but I still longed for something more. I needed a lady who'd treat me right.

Right after I got dumped I started visiting my mother a lot more. She lived about an hour away from my dad's house so it was a nice long drive to get up there, gave me time to think, to reflect on life, and to listen to tunes. My sister and her kids live with my mother, so it's always a nice trip to go up there and spend time with the family. Me and my sister made it a routine to go to the grocery store and pick up dinner whenever I went up there, and there was always this girl with short green hair who always complimented me on my nerdy T-shirts. In my mind this meant she was DIGGIN' me, so I went back at least once a week to try and hit on her. My friend Froggy worked at that grocery store, so he'd always tell me when she was around so I could go talk to her. I could never bring myself to though, I always got cold feet and she'd wind up seeing that all I liked to eat was corn dogs and fruit roll ups. Eventually, my boy Korey got me to go talk to her.

We both went to the store together, he needed Pepsi so that was our excuse for going, and when I saw her I fucking chickened out. He was like "bro what the fuck, why won't you grow a set? This isn't middle school, this is REAL LIFE." And you know what? He was right. So I went to her, and I pulled my pants up comically high, and I stuck out my finger and said "MAYBE IF YOU DON'T HAVE A BOYFRIEND WE COULD HANG OUT I GUESS?!"

Her response "LOL SORRY I HAVE A BF." GOD DAMMIT. But I fucking did it. I fucking asked a chick out. It's not that big of a deal, especially since I'd done it many times before, but still. I felt a little better about the whole situation knowing I had the balls to at least talk to a girl.

Later on I decided to try OkCupid. Not a bad site, you make a profile, post a few pictures, and message a few people to try and hang out. The first girl I got a date with wasn't bad looking, actually she kind of reminded me of Betty Boop. She was an art student, liked Resident Evil, and had a thing for cinema. Sounds like my kinda girl! We decided to hang out, go to a restaurant, and get a burger.

Let me tell you something about bad dates. She was attractive enough, but when we talked it was like I was talking to my Aunt Margaret. But here's the thing, I fucking LOVE my Aunt Margaret! That's why it's weird! It felt quasi-incestuous to be on a date with my Aunt! She wasn't that bad, really the only thing was we didn't quite connect well. So I said, fuck it, I'm gonna sabotage this date so that she doesn't wind up liking me without me liking her back.

We got on the topic of movies and she wound up asking me what my favorite film was, and she didn't seem too pleased when I mentioned that my favorite film was the 1975 classic *Salo, or The 120 Days of Sodom*, the controversial masterpiece by Pier Paolo Pasolini. When I said that I followed it up with "me and my bros like to sit around and watch this flick while getting wasted off Four Loko and eating pizza." Not only had she heard of the flick, she had SEEN it. Might I remind you that I mentioned she was somewhat of a film connoisseur, and had of course, seen that and many other great films.

I wound up being a gentleman and I paid for dinner, even though I wasn't gonna date her and she had no interest in me anyways, I didn't wanna make a college kid with no job pay. After dinner I split and headed home to the most unfortunate phone call I'd ever received. Apparently my dad and stepmom got into a drunken argument and my dad and brother left for the night and went to a hotel, and no one decided to tell me until 10:30 at night. They told me to stay with a friend or something, so I wound up going to my mom's house. There's nothing more miserable then finding out you're now homeless after you just went on the worst date of your life. Fortunately, the next day my dad and stepmom made up, but that was the last straw. Fights like that happened too often in that house, and I couldn't take it anymore. I decided I was going to move out.

But what happens when a 20 year old slacker gets his own place…

24

This is the picture I used to sell myself to the ladies in my OkCupid profile.

Destroy All Slackers

I'd never thought I'd be forced to move out of my parents' house due to the fear of being kicked out for something that had nothing to do with me. It stunk. Luckily enough my friend Josh was looking to move out of his parents' house too, so we decided to be roommates. Now I was never really close to Josh, but I knew he was an alright guy, so moving in with him and on the off chance I find myself hating him wasn't THAT big of a deal. Never move in with a close friend because if you can't live with them, you wind up hating them. This guy? Didn't care if I hated him. So we began looking for a place together like a cute married couple.

During this period I decided I didn't give a fuck about finding a girl to just date, I said fuck it. I wanted to fuck. I met this one chick named Amy who went to Ramapo College up in Mahwah who was definitely down to fuck, and wouldn't you know it she wound up being one of the coolest chicks I'd ever talk to. Her dorm was covered in Batman and Zelda posters, she was a fan of Louis C.K., and she even had the same wallpaper on her computer that I had. I can't deny that I had a crush on her, unfortunately the only thing she wanted was sex. So that's exactly what we did. Thing about this girl was that she looked exactly like this fat kid I went to middle school with and had self-inflicted cuts all over her legs just like he probably had. This same situation happened with at least two dozen other girls within this period. I was quite the busy little bee.

Anyhoo, me and Josh eventually settled on a place and November 1st we moved in and were happy little campers. For the majority of the time we lived there he was out of town, so it was more or less Kail's Poon Palace. There was a revolving door of girls coming in and having teary eyed, empty sex with me. Looking back it was pretty horrible, but at the time I felt like a drug-free Chuck Sheen! This was also when I discovered Four Loko, which I fell in love with. I'd have girls over, we'd drink some Four Loko, and before I could even bring up the idea they'd be on top of me. Unfortunately when I drink the LAST thing I want is sex. Two things I hate: drunk sex and sleep sex.

A month after I moved in, me and Teller decided to hang out one night, and we decided we were gonna do that podcast we had been talking about. We called it Destroy All Slackers, after the script I'd written months before, and our first episode was a complete success. I've told the story about how we started Destroy All Slackers a dozen times, so I'll just give you the brief skinny on it – it lead to TONS of pussy. That's a bold face lie right from my face.

Destroy All Slackers was good for me though, it showed me I really didn't need to sleep around with dozens upon dozens of girls to feel good about myself. The first few episodes had hundreds of listens, and we kept going strong for almost a year. Every week me and Teller would record ourselves acting like jackasses for the amusement of others, and it was great. I, of course, used this as a way to meet chicks.

One chick I met was really cool, her name was Bianca, she was a big Rammstein fan, and I had two tickets to the big Madison Square Garden show. I offered to take her since the person I was originally supposed to go with bailed on me (more like broke my heart, reflect back to Part 1 of this blog series), and she agreed. We'd talked for a little bit, gotten to know one another, and she was really cool. She was a little older, I was 20 and she was 26, and as it turned out she had major daddy issues.

Needless to say, I wasn't about to get my peepee slobbered OR EVEN a friendly kiss goodnight from this dame. But I still had hope!

Come the night of the show I'm texting her and calling her trying to find out what the plan is and she's not responding. Eventually she sends me a Facebook message and tells me her friend from out of town surprised her and that she'd be spending the evening with him. Just great. So I went to the show alone, unable to find someone last minute to go with me, and sat next to an empty seat the whole time. It was okay though, I got to see my favorite band and had a great time. It was an amazing show.

After the show ended I'm walking out the front of the Garden and who do I see? Bianca and her "friend" standing not five feet away from me. Immediately Biz Markie pops into my head. She comes up to me and talks to me and of course assures me he's just a friend and that she wasn't planning on sleeping with him. I may have been born at night, but I wasn't born *LAST NIGHT!* She invited me to an after party to which I politely declined, I had had my fill of fun for the night. I went home and jerked off sourly to GILF porn and then tucked myself into bed.

As December roared on, I began to find myself lonely as a pedophile in an old folk's home. I decided to try OkCupid again, maybe this time I'd find someone to hang out with who wasn't a total creep or a crazy fuck. That's when I met Kelly. We talked for a little bit online before hanging out, and she was really cool. Her only problem was that she was a little insecure about her weight, which she was a little thick, but she wore it well. It's not like she was a sloppy wale of a woman who was constantly stuffing her face with Oreos. After the freaks I've been with, a girl with a little bit of low self-esteem was a God-send.

But was I ready to commit to another relationship just yet…

This is one of the promotional pictures we used to promote the podcast. We literally called this the Fred Durst pose.

THE 120 DAYS OF BOREDOM

After Christmas me and Kelly started hanging out quite frequently, and we had a cute little romance going on. She thought I was cute and funny, I thought the things she did were endearing, it was great. We had hung out for a while and she would frequently come over the house and spend the night and we'd just chill out in my room and watch TV, it wasn't bad.

The problem was, though, was that she wanted more when I didn't. At the time I was STILL moving on after the heart break Felicia left me with, and I was also dealing with family issues that have always ate away at me, so all I wanted to do was stay in the house. She, on the other hand, wanted to go out places on dates, she wanted me to come over and hang out with her family, all stuff that seems easy enough in hindsight, but really for me at the time in my emotional state was really difficult. I was such a recluse.

There was also an anger building deep inside me at everything that had happened to me up until that point. From my point of view at the time it seemed like I could never catch a break. Looking back I was living the life, but at the time it wasn't the life I'd wanted. I'd wanted a girl I could connect with who I could hang out with and do anything with and actually be able to enjoy life, what I had though was a girl I didn't have the feelings for that she had for me and because of my anxieties I was unable to do anything.

One night that'll forever stand out in my mind as an example of how crazy I get when I feel threatened. In an effort to try and ease my way into social situations better, I decided to have a party at the apartment and invite all my boys over to meet Kelly. Sos (a frequent guest on Destroy All Slackers at that point), Teller, Josh, and a few of Josh's friends came and we just hung out and got wasted. At one point Josh was asking Kelly why she was with me, was it because of the sex or was it because she actually had feelings for me? Why he even cared is BEYOND me, but still she gave on honest answer and said that it was a little of both. He then drunkenly raged at her and yelled "THAT'S A COP OUT OF AN ANSWER!" and got right up into her face! Now up until this point every time Kelly came over she was nothing but nice to Josh, she was such a sweetheart. She was always nice to everybody, even if she didn't like them. He flipped out at her and I went nuts, but she was notably upset and I was too drunk to do anything to him, so I decided to be a gentleman and wait until people weren't around.

The next day I dropped Kelly off at her dorm and came home and flipped the fuck out at Josh. Mostly because he had left a HUGE mess in the kitchen from the night before, he had cooked a ton of meat and left it all over the place. Understandably he wouldn't clean this up while drunk, but at least do it the next morning, especially considering I'd cleaned up all the bottles and cans and other garbage everyone made. We got into a huge shouting match and he didn't even remember flipping out at Kelly the night before, but he admitted that it was possible and apologized. It was at this point that I knew I couldn't stand him, though I put up with him for the rest of our lease.

Throughout the tenure of our relationship I was pretty distant and cold from Kelly, which I feel bad for to this day. She had done nothing wrong and I'd snap at her for no reason, never anything too bad, but for example if I was listening to Opie and Anthony and they made a joke she didn't like she'd say something about it and I'd flip out at her. And there would be days where I'd go without texting her or talking to her. It's not that I wasn't interested in her, I was so numb that I just couldn't find interest in anything. After a while I felt bad for leading her on into thinking that this was gonna go anywhere, so I broke it off with her, and she was surprisingly okay with it. We would of course continue to be friends, but I couldn't keep leading her on.

About two months later I knew there was something else out there for me, so I went in search of it…

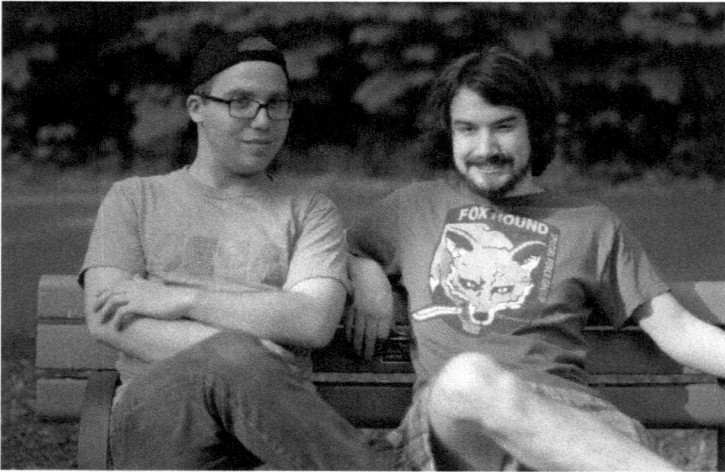

Due to the success of Destroy All Slackers, me and Teller were inseparable. I haven't talked to him much since we stopped doing the show, though, maybe I should call him soon.

THE END OF THE BEGINNING

After me and Kelly broke up I was in a state of mind where I figured it was the end. I had absolutely nothing going for me. I was even more depressed than I had been when Felicia dumped me all those months ago. Now it was worse because I didn't know what to be depressed about.

Every day was the same. I went to my shitty job, went home, watched TV, jerked off, and went to sleep. Of course, me and Teller were still doing the show, but it just didn't have that same zest that it had before. By this point we'd started interviewing some pretty cool people like Howard Drossin, a personal hero of mine, who's known for composing many classic video game soundtracks including Sonic Spinball, Comix Zone, and the recent Splatterhouse remake. We also interviewed Sonic fan film and Mega Man fan film director Eddie Lebron and his producer David S. Horowitz, which was really cool because we then became friends with them. This was all well and good, but it didn't fill me with the zest I needed to keep the ball rolling. That was when I decided to write a book.

Slacker's Paradise was to be a retrospective of all the things I'd done up till that point. I thought it was cool that I could write and perform all these songs at open mic nights, come up with an idea for a concept album that I never actually recorded, and even write an entire screenplay to a movie that would never be produced. I thought it'd also be fun for other people to get to see all the hard work I poured into all of these projects. So I began to collect all my previous works into this folder on my desktop, and I started putting it all together. One thing was missing though: personality.

I knew who I was, the listeners knew who I was, but nobody else did. How could I put out a book about someone nobody knew? So I started a blog called Slacker's Paradise on MUSCLETOWER and I posted the funniest stories I could tell about girls I'd slept with or situations I'd been in. Why not? They were funny to me, and when I told them on the show the listeners always loved them. This would compromise a good chunk of the book and be a big selling point.

While I was in the process of putting this project together, I felt a bit more confident in myself, so I decided to try OkCupid one last time. This time I sent out a hundred messages to a hundred different girls, and got only one response. This cute girl with bright blue/green eyes and long curly brown hair with tiger lily tattoos on her chest, she was absolutely gorgeous. Her name was Katie and if I told you I wasn't crazy about her the minute I first started talking to her, well I'd be telling the truth.

When we first started talking I wasn't at ALL interested in her. She had a very dry personality, and especially through talking online, the way she typed was very grammatically correct, very much like an English teacher. The main reason why I wasn't interested was because I could tell she was semi-intelligent. She was very much an actual person, rather than one of the random dime a dozen floozies I'd been sleeping around with up until that point. She was intimidating.

But, there was something about her. I couldn't quite nail it, but she intrigued me. Maybe it was because she was an actual person, or maybe it was because she shared similar wounds to the ones I had, maybe it was because she took an interest in my podcast and my comedy. I don't know what it was, but for some reason I didn't just block her from AIM and forget I ever talked to her.

After talking to her for about a month we decided to hang out, and boy was it awkward. I picked her up after nervously trying to stall the damn date the whole day and I brought her back to my house and we just watched South Park all night. What a fuckin' cassanova I am! "Excuse me, miss, but I believe I've been struck by your beauty. Would it be alright if I picked you up in my shitty little Honda Fit and brought you back to my house where we'll sit on my roommate's shitty bean bag couch and watch reruns of South Park?" Man, I'm surprised she even bothered giving me a second date.

She did, fortunately, give me a second date. And it's not because she loves South Park and horribly uncomfortable furniture. It was because she saw something in me no one else ever saw, she saw me for who I really am. She was genuinely interested in me, who I am, what I do, my interests, my comedy, etc.

And you know what? A year later and we're still together, now we even live together, and rumor has it there's gonna be a little Kail on the way soon. Everything that happened to me from the minute I had my heart broken back in September of 2010 until now has been absolutely worth it because I can honestly say I'm the happiest I've ever been. There's been bumps along the road, but like I said, it's all worth it.

As far as my comedy's concerned, I've been working with different people on different projects, a few botched attempts at an internet talk show, I wrote a BOOK, I'm always making people laugh on Twitter still, I'll always be updating the DudeGurlz site with my thoughts on life, and I'll always be chasing the dream of Gurlz, Lunch, and Money.

As Chris (Simpsons artist) would say – Reach for the stars, you idiot!

CHAPTER 2

BLOGS - PART 1

MY QUEST FOR FOURTH MEAL

Last night I saw a commercial for Taco Bell's Beefy Crunch Burrito and I said "Holy shit, I need to have that in my gullet right this second." This is what happened after.

My girlfriend Katie was sick as a dog all day yesterday, the doctor said she had a stomach virus and that it'd go away in 24 hours, but those 24 hours were Hell. I left work early to take care of her, and I was constantly running all over Hackensack looking for medicine and drinks she could drink and food she could eat etc. It was a pain in the butt, to say the least.

I wound up having a late lunch, so when I made her chicken soup for dinner I didn't bother making myself anything because I wasn't hungry. One thing led to another, I wind up busy the rest of the night working on my upcoming talk show, and I lost track of the time. Around 10 we're watching Family Guy and on comes a commercial for Taco Bell.

I see this commercial, and as it's supposed to do, it gets me in the mood for Fourth Meal. I ask Katie if she's in the mood for Taco Bell and she looks at me like I have three god damn heads. "Are you crazy?" She says, "I could BARELY eat the soup you made me! How am I going to stomach Taco Bell?"

Shot down. Feels bad man. But maybe there's a way. I could justify going out for Fourth Meal if I can make it a productive trip. I ask her if there's anything she needs and she goes "Well, some ginger ale would be nice."

So now I had a reason to leave the house that didn't make me feel like a fat, worthless piece of shit. I put on my coat, grabbed my wallet and keys, hopped in the car, put on some Offspring, and I sped off like a bat out of Hell.

First I stopped at Quick Check, which is a convenience store I mentioned in my book Slacker's Paradise. Y'see, when I first moved to Hackensack I had a huge crush on the chick behind the counter here. Not really, I just thought she was hot. I made a mention of her in my book, and when I walked in she saw me and gave me a look like she knew I had written about her in my book. Hey, lady, it's not like I wrote about every lasting fantasy I had for you! Hmmm... maybe I should do that, just to fuck with her. Anyhoo, I'm off track. So I grab Katie's shit and I bounce the fuck out of there because I had big dreams of big eats.

Now I'm strollin' down the road headed towards paradise, I'm singin' as loud as I can to the music, I'm in a fantastic mood. I was happier than Jerry Sandusky when he stumbled into the "Boys Pants Half Off" section of Kohl's.

I pull up to the drive through window and the woman over the intercom asks me for my order. I tell her "Lemme get a Beefy Crunch Burrito combo." She says "Hard or soft taco?" in reference to the two tacos the combo comes with, I respond "SOFT TACO, NO LETTUCE." I said it as clear as a beautiful sunny day in the Jersey Shore, and I'm not talking about Snooki's acne ridden ass-cheeks.

I pull up to the window, hand them my debit card, take my food, get my card back, and head home. I briefly looked in the bag, it looked like my order, so I put it on the passenger seat and blasted some Volbeat.

I got home and whipped open the bag, tossed Katie her shit, and began going to town on my burrito. BUT WAIT! What's this? HARD SHELL TACO, TONS OF LETTUCE.

WHAT. THE. FUCK.

I didn't order this shit! In fact, they specifically asked me if I wanted hard or soft taco! HARD OR SOFT TACO! I TOLD THEM SOFT! NO LETTUCE! WHYYYYYYYYYY!!!!!

Needless to say I was pissed. For the rest of the night I was cranky. Katie was feeling better, but I wasn't. I could've just gone back out and gotten them to fix it, but it was already 10:30 and Taco Bell is like a 15 minute drive from my house. It was almost pointless. I had been fucked. Royally.

Thanks, Taco Bell. You ruined my night.

42

Super Mario - Middle Aged Menace

Super Mario is a grown man, probably in his late 30's, early 40's. Nintendo has somehow made a franchise that's incredibly profitable and extremely popular with children about someone who could very well be one of their fathers or authority figures. Why is it so popular?

Let's take a look at the character and the franchise as a whole. Mario is a human male, rather short for a dude, let's assume he's about 5'4". He's a licensed plumber from Brooklyn with a curly handlebar mustache, blue denim overalls, brown work shoes, a red long sleeve shirt with white gloves (work gloves stylized to look cartoonish), and a red hat with a stylized M on the front (a possible logo for his plumbing business). The generally accepted plot of the whole franchise is that Mario and his younger, but taller, brother Luigi get warped from their home in modern day Brooklyn to the fantastic Mushroom Kingdom, which is a cartoonish kingdom in the style of Alice in Wonderland, in fact, we can say this entire series was influenced by Alice in Wonderland in one way or another. While in the Mushroom Kingdom they meet Princess Toadstool, a.k.a Peach, and she gets kidnapped by the evil King Koopa, a.k.a. Bowser, who has unsavory intentions for her (be it holding her ransom in exchange for control of the kingdom as the self-applied King in his name would imply, or maybe he wants a wife, or maybe he wants to rape her). Mario and Luigi are joined by their friends Yoshi and Toad to fight in the battle of good against evil.

The series originally started as a more-or-less rip-off of Popeye with an arcade game called "Donkey Kong." Mario creator Shigeru Miyamoto had wanted to make a video game adaptation of the Popeye series which involved the hero Popeye fighting the villainous Bluto in an attempt to save the maiden Olive Oil, but he could not secure the rights from Paramount to put together such a game. What then occurred was the idea of taking the Popeye formula (average Joe hero fights large, stupid doofus to rescue the girl of his dreams) and throw in his own characters. Instead of Spinach eating Popeye the Sailor Man we got the carpenter Jumpman (later renamed Mario), who's design consisted of a hat to cover the fact that Miyamoto couldn't animate hair, overalls to make animating arm movements easier, and a mustache to help distinguish the nose from his face. Instead of the macho jerk Bluto we're given Donkey Kong, Jumpman's pet gorilla, who gives us our large, stupid villain, and as our damsel in distress we're given Pauline, a more 1980's style sex symbol who's arguably more attractive than Olive Oil could ever be. The idea here was to appeal to all audiences with a timeless story of a regular Joe, someone the player could relate to, fighting to save his girlfriend from a rampaging gorilla. The success of Donkey Kong inevitably lead to sequels and the return of Mario.

In 1985 Nintendo released the Family Computer (Famicom) in Japan and Shigeru Miyamoto wanted to bring his Mario character to the system in a new way. With a new system that was arguably more powerful than what he worked with in the arcades he had new ideas he wanted to implement in his games, thus he gave Mario the ability to grow with mushrooms and other abilities from other power-ups for the "Super" Mario series, and he put him in a fantastical world unlike the Brooklyn setting of the arcade games. This is where things started to get strange, as now console games are less for everyone and are more for the kids in the family.

Mario's original success in Donkey Kong was due to the fact that people could relate to the character, and for the first time in a video game we were given something of a narrative. By the time of the NES when Super Mario Bros. was released, we really didn't have much to relate to, and while it's always exciting to explore new terrain, see things you wouldn't see in real life, it's just really strange to me that the character that children take on the persona of to do this exploring is that of a middle-aged, Italian-American plumber.

That's the point of this blog post. Take the character out of the equation and really study him, as I did at the beginning. He's literally a middle-aged Italian-American plumber from Brooklyn, a man who could be any kid's father, a possible authority figure. I remember being a kid and wanting to be like Bart Simpson, wanting to rebel against authority, wanting to be a kid who can show what he's made of. My nephew feels the same way, he loves movies like The Goonies where kids go on fantastic adventures against all odds.

How does a character such as Mario become such a hit to the extent where a game that came out in 2006 (New Super Mario Bros., NDS) is still charting today in the Top 20. What about New Super Mario Bros. Wii? That's been in the Top 20 since it came out. Any Mario Kart game is automatically a top of the charts hit.

But what about him is appealing to children? Well, take a look at his current character model. He looks more like a boy with a mustache now than what he actually is. Big blue eyes, soft pale skin, welcoming smile, jolly pot belly, cast of friends who all invite you to join their group. That's the game Nintendo's been playing, give the middle aged man a younger look, when the character first debuted he looked older, now he looks almost like a young teenager.

Personally, I'm a huge fan of the Super Mario franchise. Why do I love the games? The gameplay. It's fun, addicting, simple, and engaging. Maybe that's why these games sell so much, because despite the fact that parents should be weary of their children playing as a middle aged man with a hideous mustache, these games still sell millions. Based on gameplay alone. That's a spicy meat-a ball!

MY LUCKY SOCIAL DISTORTION T-SHIRT

Everyone's got something that gives them luck, for me it happens to be this gray Social Distortion T-shirt that I got from the discount rack at Hot Topic. What makes it so lucky? I honestly have no idea, but for some reason I wear it whenever I feel like I need a boost of luck.

I got the shirt on a whim back when I was dating my ex Felicia because she worked at Hot Topic and I could use the discount. My general rule of thumb is when someone you're dating buys you something, once the relationship is over you can no longer use it, so if you're sweetie got you a pacemaker and you suddenly find yourself dumped, you gotta give up your life. Sorry, those are the rules. I paid for the shirt myself so I get to still wear it, regardless of whether or not I took advantage of her totally sweet discount (which I THINK was nearly 50% off shirts, not sure though, wouldn't be surprised considering the ridiculous mark-up stores like that put on their shirts.) Anyhoo, she dumped me and now I suddenly had a whole wardrobe of clothes to throw the fuck out because she'd come home with new shirts every week for me. It was more like two or three shirts, but lucky for me I was able to keep my Social D shirt because I'd thrown down my own hard earned sponduli for it.

During the awkward phase where I was still trying to get over her, but dating around, I wound up landing myself a date with a sweet girl named Chrissy. She was short, maybe about five foot even, had really short curly jet black hair, curvy body, and glasses similar to mine. She was my type at the time, which was short girls with short hair and glasses. We met online, talked a little, found each other endearing, and then the time came to actually hang out and we set up a date at the Rockaway Mall to just walk around and get to know each other. Best piece of advice I can give you on getting to know someone is by walking around a mall, by doing this you can casually talk as you walk through stores and you can get a feel for what they may be into by the stores they want to go in and the things they look at.

In getting prepared for this date I decided I was gonna go all out. Black Castro hat, red flannel shirt, gray corduroys, and my lucky Social Distortion shirt. I didn't think I needed the luck, because from the way she was talking to me on AIM and through text I could see she was totally into me, at this point it was all about closing the deal. You guys know my rule: ABC - Always Be Closing.

I arrived at the mall and I was so nervous about meeting her, I sent her a text and asked where she was and she said she was at a calendar kiosk where her cousin worked. Awkwardly enough for me, I got to meet both her and her cousin at the same time. What made things easier on me was the fact that her cousin had recognized me, which suddenly boosted my cool points. She'd apparently seen me perform a couple times when I played shows, and she thought I was funny. This impressed Chrissy, and now I suddenly had my confidence. We left her cousin and strolled along through the mall and talked, we'd go into this store, we'd go into that store, and I saw an awesome Sonic pillow case at FYE that I was totally gonna buy, but wound up feeling self-conscious because she laughed at how childish it was. This would be a recurring theme of the night, her finding my mannerisms very childish and my catch-phrases even worse.

The whole night she was holding my hand and going in and holding my arm, but at the same time hating my personality, I couldn't tell what the dealio is. Eventually, I was just like "Yeah, I'm gonna go home now, I got work in the morning." and I walked her to her car. I went to give her a hug, thinking this date didn't really go anywhere but it was still okay enough where we were friendly, and she went in and kissed me. In my book, when a girl kisses you on the lips it generally means she's got the hots for you. That's what I assumed, so I said goodbye and left and felt like a million bucks.

Over the next few days she would wind up texting me with mixed feelings about the whole thing. One day she'd be really into me and tell me she'd dreamed about me the night before, another day she'd be annoyed at the fact that I was texting her at all. It eventually got to be too much and I laid it out for her.

"Are you actually interested in me or what? I don't mind taking things slow, but I just want to know if there's anything to this." I said to her defiantly over AIM where I could be Mr. Toughguy behind the safety of the screen.

"I really don't know..." she said back.

"Well, when you do know, give me a call. I like you, but I'm not going to keep chasing you if one day you're all super into me and the next day you hate my guts." Really, the cooler thing would've been for me to call her gay as hell and block the fuck out of her.

What was the point of this story again? Oh yeah, my lucky shirt. Turns out it wasn't so lucky after all, I mean the shirt did magically inspire her to kiss me on the lips, but I didn't get to close the deal. That was the closest thing to this shirt ever being considered lucky, every other time I wore it nothing really happened. A couple times I got laid, but that was mostly because I'd been suave and fucking handsome as all Hell, and the girls had been loose and desperate.

Funny side note, my first date with my current girlfriend Katie I figured was going to be a bust. I absolutely did not think there was a chance in the world that I would've liked her or that she would've liked me, it just wasn't going to happen. So to avoid the frustration of wasting my lucky Social Distortion shirt on her, I wore this Hawaiian Punch shirt I'd had that I barely ever wore. I also threw in a CD of songs I never listened to in my car because I didn't want to stain any of my favorite jams with what could've possibly been the worst date ever. Well, as you all know, me and Katie are happily in love and we live together.

I still don't wear that Hawaiian Punch shirt, and the Social Distortion shirt always gets first pick if I'd just done the laundry.

The shirt in question, don't I look wonderful?

FULL HOUSE BEGINS

There have been a mess of great TV shows being adapted as feature films in recent years, some worse than others, but one film has gone untouched for many years, until now. I present you all with an excerpt from my latest screenplay - the opening scene from my adaptation of the wonderful family sitcom Full House.

INT. SCENE – TANNER FAMILY LIVING ROOM

Christmas Morning. Uncle Joey wakes up bright and early at the crack of dawn and as he walks in through the kitchen entrance he stretches his arms and lets out a pleasant yawn to let the world know he's awake and ready to open presents.

He begins to sing.

UNCLE JOEY [SINGING]:

Ohhhhhhh, what a beautiful morning!

He struts forth, arms out and all, making a
Popeye face while murmuring to himself in true
Popeye fashion.

UNCLE JOEY [POPEYE VOICE]:
Ooh, will you lookit that! Ug, ug-ug-ug-ug, ug!

He then notices something amiss in the middle of
the living room. A look of distress immediately
consumes his face. The look evokes a mixture of
shock, disgust, and horror.

As the sun rises and sunshine peers through the
windows, we see the horrors that happened not
moments before.

DJ's corpse lies in the center of the family
living room, half eaten and torn apart on top of
the coffee table that sits between the couch and
TV set.

In the corner of the room near the staircase, we
see DJ's longtime boyfriend Steve hunched over
with his back to the camera. Loud crunching
noises are heard coming from him. Uncle Joey
attempts to figure out what happened.

UNCLE JOEY:
Steve? Steve… is that you?

Steve turns his head slowly, looking over his
shoulder towards Uncle Joey. His eyes are pure
white, like those of a demon, and his face

resembles that of an animal that's just struck down it's pray. During the process of turning he reveals that he was eating DJ's arm which he previously tore off her body.

Before he has the chance to scream, Steve howls at Uncle Joey and leaps towards him. Midway through the leap the camera freezes on the scene and a red filter slowly sets in as the camera zooms in on the frozen scene. "Midnight Rider" by The Allman Brothers Band begins to play as the opening credits roll.

FULL HOUSE.

PIZZA

When I was a kid living in Paterson, NJ in the early 90's we used to order from Little Caesar's pizza, and throughout my childhood whenever my mom took me to K-Mart we would always eat at the Little Caesar's within the store.

Throughout the 80's Little Caesars was known for their two large pizzas for $8.98 deal, which is remarkable today considering one large pizza is like $12. In 1999 you could get a cheese pizza and a large soda at Panucci's Pizza for $10.77 (same as my pin number), but now? Little more costly. Though Pizza Hut offers any large one topping pizza for only $10, plus ridiculous taxes and hidden fees (welcome to Obama's America).

I haven't had Little Caesars in I don't know HOW long, maybe ten years. The last time I actually shopped at a K-Mart was June 2002. I'll never forget that day, I'd made $100 selling Pokémon cards or some shit, I forget how I came into $100, but I wanted to spend it on GameCube games. My mom took me to K-Mart, and I wound up buying Bomberman Generations (which sucked) and a few Gundam model kits. You need to remember, at this point in history Gundam was a very valid anime and model kits were available in actual stores, not just specialty shops. Anyhoo, we had eaten at the Little Caesars at the K-Mart that day, and it was spectacular. I miss my mommy, maybe I'll call her up soon.

Back on topic, tonight I decided to take a look and see where there might be a Little Caesars by me that isn't in a K-Mart. I found one in Union City, but if you know New Jersey you know not to go around there at night, especially if you're white. It's not Camden bad, but it's not a real safe place. I checked Google Street View to see if it was ACTUALLY there, and to my surprise Street View brought me to a Dunkin Donuts/Baskin Robbins. That's not Little Caesars! I wasn't about to chance going into Union City after dark, so I decided to scrap those plans for tonight.

But what about some other pizzas? Pizza Hut, Papa Johns, Dominos, all great choices. I've had them all, loved them all. Chuck E Cheese and Cici's are other great pizza choices. Stuffed crust meat lovers from Pizza Hut is my personal favorite, but I also enjoy a 5-5-5 deal from Dominos. Papa Johns is just straight up delicious, though. Every time I eat Pizza Hut I get massive amounts of diarrhea, but it's okay because it's SO good I just can't stop.

Cici's kinda stinks because the pizza's so thin and it's mostly crust so they really cut corners on the actual pizza. Since it's a pizza buffet you get full after a few slices, which is kind of a scam, but whatever, I don't go there anymore. Chuck E. Cheese is mad good if you're a kid. As an adult I enjoy the taste, but it's just not filling enough to warrant me giving a damn. Plus a grown man can't just go to Chuck E. Cheese and sit down with a slice and enjoy the live stage show, that's a bit weird. I think they literally have a rule where you can't come in unless accompanied by a child anyways. I know playgrounds usually have that rule, especially in New York. You ever try to go to a playground just to have a good time with yourself and get thrown out because you're a grown man without a child? Again, welcome to Obama's America!

I remember Pizza Hut used to have a great mascot, it was like a pizza puppet guy named pizza head or something. He was an annoying little shit, and he didn't look appealing. As a kid you want fucking pepperoni, sausage, bacon, ham, not like peppers and lettuce and shit. Salads are for girls and homosexual men. Fuck salads.

I hope you enjoyed my thoughts on pizza, because I enjoyed speaking about pizza. I hate the greasy feel of pizza because if I masturbate after enjoying a friendly slice I get crazy pimples on my dick. It's not an STD, it's just from eating greasy pizza, no big deal.

60

KAIL'S GUIDE TO PROPER DATING ETIQUETTE

This is something I wrote back in 2009 as a goof on my personal Facebook page. Notice how my writing style doesn't match my current style, that's because at the time I wasn't much of a writer. I thought it was funny so I decided to include it in this book. It's essentially how to pick up gurlz by a guy who's never seen a pussy before in his life. Truth be told up until this point I'd only been with like two or three girls, so I was in no position to be giving anyone advice. If you can successfully use this as a guide to picking up women, then you're a better man than I.

This is a guide to all the Michael Ceras out there who don't know how to properly woo a woman, or even get a girl to talk to you. I wrote this from my own past experience, because even though I can't seem to find a girl I'm interested in enough to pursue in an actual relationship, I can seem to find several girls that are attracted to me for whatever reason (be it that they just wanna hook up, or they actually like me, usually they just want to hook up).

First thing you gotta do, take a god damn shower, make yourself look presentable. A t-shirt and jeans will do, just make sure they're washed, make sure you're clean, and you gotta smell good. Wear deodorant! Also, you need an actual smell, not just deodorant. Sometimes AXE can be a little overkill, but if you got it, use it, don't spray it on yourself, you silly man, spray it in front of you and walk into the cloud. Not too much though, you don't wanna smell like you're trying too hard. Don't have AXE? No problem, head down to where Mom keeps the febreze and spray yourself a little with that, one of my friends (not gonna say who to protect their identity) does that and I started doing it and it works, you smell great, you're not boring, you're now good to go!

Now that you're smelling good and looking good, you gotta get some confidence in you. Chances are if you haven't been with a girl, you're a Dragon Ball Z fan. Think back to when Piccolo would train by himself, he would split into separate Piccolos and would fight himself. Take that concept and try it out. In your mind, envision yourself splitting into two, now make one of those yourself, the one that controls the body, and the other is a motivator who tells you what to do. Prep yourself a couple hours before you go out to a spot where the girls who are looking to meet new people are(don't just walk up to anyone, you're not ready for that yet), and have the motivator tell you that you're going to talk to a girl.

Confidence is now all yours, you look good, you smell good, you got your game face on, I think you're ready for the party! When going to a party, keep in mind that if you do get with any of the girls there, chances are they're not looking for a relationship, they're just looking for some attention for the night. Party girls often come from broken families or they have problems at home and are just looking to escape, don't try to help them, they have one thing on their mind for the night and that's not charity from some guy with Febreze on his chest, it's booze and dudez.

Ok so you're at the party, you spy a girl you think is cute, first thing is first, have your motivator tell you to go for it, and now you don't wanna disappoint your motivator, so you have to go for it. Go up to her and say "Hi, I'm [your name here], what's your name?" If she gives you a name, you're basically in for at least a good conversation, if not, go to the next girl on your list. Let's say she gave you a name (it might not be her real name, but that's not important, she's probably not a keeper anyways), now you gotta kick start the conversation. But before you do that, the music in the room is too loud, ask her if she wants to go somewhere where you guys can talk, if she says yes, then you're golden! Now go somewhere where the music isn't so loud and talk to her. First rule: DO NOT talk to her only about you, let her think she's in control of the conversation, ask her what she's in to and let her dictate the flow of the conversation, eventually she'll ask you about yourself and it's at this point that you have her interested enough to wanna know about you, which is where you're in the lead. Don't talk too much, leave a little mystery to you, let her talk for about 70% of the conversation this way she feels comfortable and you don't have to work so hard to impress her. If you're not talking, chances are you're not saying something you'll soon regret.

If everything is going well at this point, which it should unless you're going for girls who are either too shallow to deal with you or just aren't interested, then you might be getting a kiss tonight! SCORE! At this point, there's nothing else you can really do, the situation will just go along as it is and will only go up hill from here. Things to keep in mind: don't be nervous, girls really can sense fear, trust me, I know. Just be cool, calm, and collective. Don't be too loud either, and don't get too excited. If you get too excited, you may do something you might regret, and she will probably lose interest and think you're an idiot. Once you get past that first introduction though, you should be golden the rest of the ride. Congratulate yourself, as you've just gotten some. How does it feel? Bet it feels pretty good, eh?

Would you believe I never walked up and talked to a girl I didn't know until I had already graduated high school? Now I haven't been with a lot of girls, but I have been with my fair share, more than enough really. While it's important to only give away your proverbial goods to the one you're sure you have real feelings for, meeting a girl at a party and hooking up isn't necessarily a bad thing.

Now as my final words, this process will not find you love, it will only help boost your confidence when it comes to talking to girls and attracting them. As you can see, I'm still single, and probably will be for a long time. Not because I can't land a girlfriend, but because I can't find one I'm really interested in. Don't settle for just anyone, go for someone you're at least attracted to and you think you'd be good in a relationship with.

Good luck with getting with MMMMMMM GURLZ!

Derek, Myself, and the man who taught me all I know about getting with the ladies.

WHO TOUCHES THE WATCHMEN?

The following is an opinion piece I wrote about the then-upcoming Before Watchmen prequel series. I wrote this the day after the news broke out because in the 24 hours between I found out and I wrote this, a complete shit-storm of fanboyism took over the internet with numerous fans crying foul over DC touching Alan Moore's masterpiece. By the time this book is published the storm will probably have already passed and for all I know Before Watchmen could be as well regarded as the original. It'd be really funny if it wasn't and I was completely wrong. Imagine that? There would be public record of me being a moron as this book is PUBLISHED and IN STORES. Anyhoo, enjoy.

This has been hot news for the past day or two, and in the time between me first reading about it and now I've been able to form an opinion on how I feel on this. DC's attempt to make a prequel series to Alan Moore's 1985 hit Watchmen called Before Watchmen is going to be awesome.

For the past few months every so often a rumor would pop up about a possible Watchmen 2 or a prequel of some sorts, and even when accompanied by some concept art which would be removed instantly due to cease and desist orders from DC, we still wouldn't believe it. It's just too out there. Watchmen is the holy grail of comics. It's the perfect story told in comic book form, it alone gave credibility to the entire comic book industry and the medium itself. But is it really all that and a bag of chips?

Look at what Watchmen is on the surface. A graphic novel telling the story of a group of retired costumed heroes, a mystery surrounding the death of a prominent and controversial former costumed hero, and the on-going struggles between America and the USSR in an alternate 1985. The characters are interesting, the story is engaging, and for the most part it is a self-contained story that has a solid beginning, middle, and end. If Watchmen had come out today it would be very popular, but it wouldn't have made the impact it made 25 years ago.

Now let's look at how the comics world sees Watchmen. It's considered the single greatest graphic novel ever written, and it's received numerous awards since it was first published. The characters have become icons in their own right, standing not for comic books, but instead for the importance of storytelling in comic books. Unlike Batman, which is a product of DC Comics, Watchmen is the words of Alan Moore and the art of Dave Gibbons. With Batman anyone can write a story and it's considered canon to some universe, but Watchmen exists only in the universe of Alan Moore and Dave Gibbons and cannot, and WILL not, fit anywhere else. Why is that? Why do we constantly fight that what can be done to Batman and Superman can't be done to Watchmen? Why COULDN'T there be a sequel to Watchmen?

Well, there can't be a reasonable sequel to Watchmen considering (SPOILER) the best character dies at the end of the book, Dr. Manhattan leaves the galaxy, the Comedian is still dead, and we're left with the two worst, most selfish, and more importantly most UNINTERESTING characters in the history of comics (Silk Spectre II and Nite Owl II). They're good characters because everyone else works off of them, but alone they're fucking idiots.(END SPOILER) To do a sequel and have it be interesting you'd have to either introduce all-new characters and essentially remake Kick-Ass, focus on characters that are completely uninteresting, or bring back everyone that ruled through some nonsensical plot element. It couldn't be done. A prequel on the other hand? Well, the book was just chock full of flashbacks and allusions to stories that previously happened. How could you not do a prequel when the book itself paints a guide for which you could work off of?

Within the very pages of the original Watchmen lies the blueprint from which a prequel could be devised, such as when Nite Owl and Rorschach mention that they were once partners in crime fighting, Ozymandias alluding to his many adventures and then retiring from crime fighting to start an empire, Silk Spectre II being forced to fight crimes by her mother, it's all there in the book itself. Anyone who says a prequel couldn't work is an absolute moron because Moore himself has stated numerous times that he wanted to do a whole Minutemen prequel that dealt with the older heroes.

People argue that Moore's original vision shouldn't be touched and that Watchmen should be left as is, and to them I say why? Look, I respect Moore and his works, but the truth is that these are comic books, it's not like they're tampering with the Bible, or even worse, changing history by altering text books. Someone might be doing that, but DC Comics isn't. I don't know that, but I'm assuming that. Anyways, point is the original Watchmen is being left alone, they're not pulling a George Lucas and fucking with the original graphic novel so that they can make a sequel or do a prequel any differently. The original Watchmen is being left as-is, and the people working on the prequel series are fans of the original work.

Speaking of which, who do we have working on Before Watchmen? Brian Azzarello, Darwyn Cooke, J. Michael Straczynski and original Watchmen editor Len Wein are writing, while Cooke, Lee Bermejo, Amanda Conner, Adam Hughes, J.G. Jones, Andy and Joe Kubert, Jae Lee and original Watchmen colorist John Higgins are doing the art. Those are LEGENDARY names in the field of comics, names that respect the works of Alan Moore and Dave Gibbons, and respect and understand the very nature of Watchmen. Hell, even the editor and colorist from the original graphic novel are working on it. If anyone involved understands Watchmen, it's them, and you'll be damn sure they'll smack some sense into the others if they don't adhere to the original book.

But WHY is DC Comics doing this? Why now? This would've been a more appropriate publicity stunt during promotion of the 2009 movie when "Watchmenia" was at its height, but here we are 3 years later in 2012 and most people either don't remember or choose to forget the film adaptation by Zak Snyder. I myself enjoyed it immensely, but that's neither here nor there. The reason might not seem to be so apparent, but really look at what's going on at DC Comics right now. Aside from Batman, their movies don't do so well, whereas Marvel's film division is flourishing. They recently cancelled all their on-going comic series and rebooted them all in an event that was called "The New 52". They even just announced a new "series" of logos to replace the 2005 DC logo that focus on the identity of the comic rather than the DC corporation.

Usually when a company wants to increase interest in their properties and drive up sales, they'll do a cross-over event of some sort where all their characters team up to stop an unspeakable evil and in the process one of the most popular characters dies (only to come back shortly thereafter). This happens yearly in the comics world, and frankly I feel it's a tired practice. These "events" only serve to drive readers nuts, as to follow them you have to buy literally every comic in the event's series as well as several issues of individual series just to get a basic grasp on what's going on. In a business sense, this Watchmen prequel idea is a great move considering you're taking characters that HAVEN'T been visited in 25 years and telling their individual stories in a big way. This could be seen as 2012's "event" for DC comics, and I think it's great because you don't have to start buying comics you don't read just to understand it. This itself is a self-contained story in as much the same way as the original Watchmen was self-contained.

To be honest, I have no problem with them doing this. Just like I had absolutely no problem with Fox doing a movie adaptation of Dragon Ball that wound up being a horrible mess. Whether this turns out to be a good thing worthy of being excited about or not is yet to be seen, so far all we have is some really cool cover art. If that's any indication on how the prequel series is to be handled, then yes, I do think this is something to celebrate. I'm all for this Watchmen prequel series and I even celebrate them doing it. And just like the Star Wars prequels, at the end of the day we still have the original, but unlike Star Wars our original series will be left untouched.

GINGERS

Growing up people often times expressed vibrantly how much they loved my red hair. Older women I didn't know were quick to grab me and pull me close to them for an embarrassingly painful hug while yelling to the world about how cute I was and how much they loved my hair. Other people, however, weren't so friendly.

Race, religion, culture, gender, interests, outward appearance, these are all things people should not be judged for. People should not be judged, people should not be degraded, people should not be harassed for any of the above. Unfortunately, it happens. What're you supposed to do about it? The thing is, though, is that no one escapes from it. Everyone, at one point in their life, is ridiculed for something about them they can't help.

For me, that one thing was being a red head, and it didn't start until Thursday, November 6th, 2005. The latest episode of South Park had debuted the night before, and while I'd stopped watching South Park mostly when the phenomenon started to wane in the very early 2000's, other kids at school still watched it. The episode was titled "Ginger Kids", and that's exactly what it was about. It was bound to happen eventually, as it does to everyone, and finally it did. Trey and Matt did an episode about my people.

My whole life people adored my red hair, nobody ever made me feel bad about it. Sure I got the occasional "carrot top" when they didn't have anything left to throw at me, but I'd never seen anything like this. The episode was a satire on hate speech, Cartman gave a presentation about "Gingervitis" being a disease that turns normal kids into soul-less gingers. Trey and Matt actually had good intentions this time around, they used the idea that red-heads were different as a plot device to show how ignorant people could be, unfortunately the fantasy of the show became a reality.

Starting November 6th, 2005 every day at school I had to deal with people coming up to me and calling me a ginger kid and claiming I had no soul. Every time I'd raise my hand to answer a question someone would make a joke about gingers, and sometimes even the teachers would get involved. You'd think this is grossly inappropriate, but the unfortunate reality is unless you're a REAL minority (black, gay, Jewish, female, etc.) your opinion doesn't matter. That's a bit of a stretch, but really you go to someone and say "I was made fun of because I have red hair", they're gonna look at you like you have three heads. The blacks were once slaves, the Jews had been persecuted for thousands of years for their beliefs, women have been treated as less than men since the dawn of time, you're complaining just because some kids watched South Park and are now picking on you?

The term ginger comes from British-English slang and over there is usually derogatory, but in their culture if you don't pull a gun on someone and shoot them until they're dead it's not really a big deal. Because of this, hipster friends of mine who enjoy British culture (aka jerkoff kids who watch the British version of The Office, Doctor Who, Misfits, etc.) would call me a ginger and say "no, it's not mean, it's what the British refer to red-heads as, so it's okay." Really? Is me calling Will Smith a nigger okay? Because that's what my great grandfather probably would've referred to him as.

Do I get routinely offended by the term? I get offended when the person using the term is ignorant of how it makes someone else feel. Even then, I don't get offended, I just get annoyed.

But Kail, you routinely make derogatory jokes about people of different races, cultures, genders, etc. What makes you so special? Well, Sherlock, I'm a comedian. I don't open up in casual conversation with people I'm not really close with and start saying "well, I can't wait for Holocaust 2 to happen, and I hope it happens to the nigger, chinks, spics, gooks, and Jews (again)", I don't even get that strong in my comedy. I usually avoid racial slurs unless a specific joke calls for it, or I'm going for the shock of saying "nigger". I'm no shock comic, but a good shocking joke every now and again doesn't hurt.

The point of this blog wasn't to express my distaste at the whole "gingers" thing, but more to point out how Trey Parker and Matt Stone tried to satirize the ignorance of modern man, and instead created a new way to hate a group of people. Do I condemn them? No, I condemn anyone idiot enough to take South Park any way other than it's intended to be taken. Like a moron who breaks his neck mimicking a stunt from Jackass, anyone who imitates anything from South Park obviously isn't all that intelligent.

Like I said, at one point or another it happens to literally everybody. It's human nature to fear those that are different from us, and we deal with fear through different ways. We deal with fear through laughing about it nicely, attacking it maliciously, or learning about how and why it's different. Most people go for the first two options, not realizing there's a third. Myself? I learn about it, and laugh about it. We're all different, but really, we're all the same.

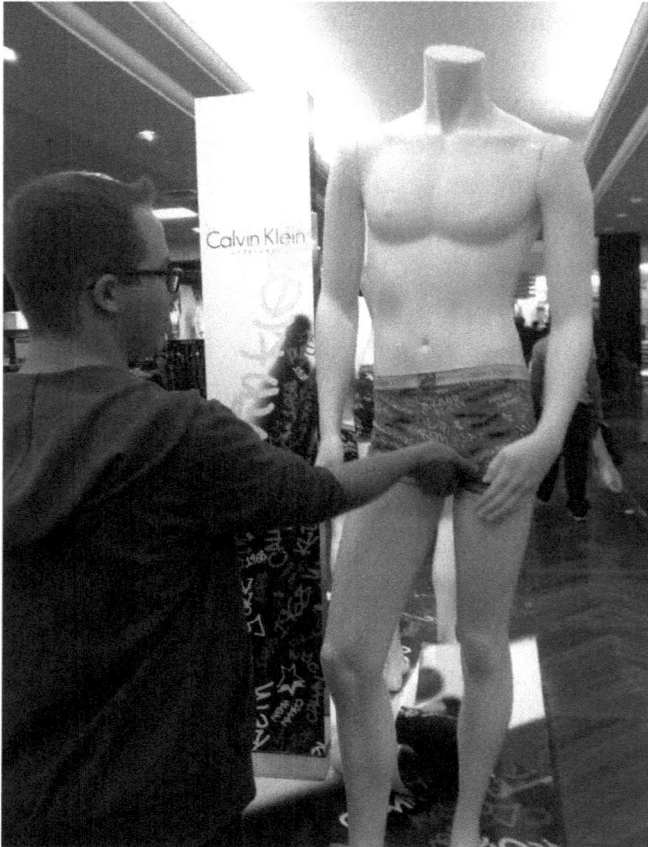

Red seems to be my preferred color of choice. If you're color blind or a dog then this picture won't make sense to you.

How I Would Reboot the Back to the Future Franchise

There's no question about it, the Back to the Future trilogy is quite possibly the greatest trilogy of all time. It's up there against Star Wars and Lord of the Rings. Unfortunately, we live in a dystopian society where originality in film is looked down upon and everything has to be a rehash of something else. Well, here's how I'd make my big splash in the film industry: by rebooting the Back to the Future trilogy to fit a modern setting.

You see, Back to the Future is a very dated film series, not dated in the sense that it's showing its age, because really it's a timeless classic, but Back to the Future's "Present" is 1985. It's currently 2012. Sometimes you have to make creative decisions in the reboot process, and my reboot would be no different, so I will be setting it in the year of 2015. That's so I can tie it in to the original trilogy, and because by the time the film is made it'll be released in 2015 (the wheels are turning as we speak, right now I'm shaking hands and signing agreements left and right).

The first film in my trilogy would be about a 17 year old Marty McFly in the year 2015, he loves 90's grunge, playing guitar, chasing girls, skateboarding, and similar timeless boyhood activities. He works a part time job as assistant to Dr. Emmett L. Brown, aka "Doc," who doubles as his best friend, but he mostly spends his time surfing the internet for hilarious pictures of cats. One day the Doc shows him a fucking cool as hell DeLorean time machine, and Marty, having been born in 1998, asks him what the fuck that shit is. The Doc slaps him and says "mind your god damn manners, it's a classic car designed by a drug peddling criminal." He then explains how it's a time machine that can travel through time like nobody's business, so Marty has this brilliant idea to go back in time to the year 2000 to introduce cats to the internet and make a cool million for himself. Doc gets shot by some heroin dealer he ripped the car off of, and Marty makes his escape to the past with a car full of screaming cats.

While in the far off year of 2000 A.D. he meets a younger version of his father who's being bullied by some asshole named Jim Davis. Jim is constantly calling Marty's dad George names like "candyass" and "faggot" and he loves listening to Limp Bizkit, whereas George listens to the score from Star Wars on his Diamond Rio MP3 player. Believe it or not, he can fit ten tracks on that thing! Marty fucking lays Jim out in the middle of a diner and tells George about his idea to fuck bitches and get money by posting pictures of cats on the internet. The two work together and become internet billionaires with Marty changing his name to Marty Dotcom.

I'm a respectable man who doesn't like to think too far ahead, but I'm pretty confident that this film will clean the house at the Oscars. After winning nearly every Oscar, just losing out to Best Score because I refuse to work with Hans Zimmer (personal reasons, please, don't be rude), Universal decides to give me every gold brick in Fort Knox to make a sequel. Unbeknownst to them, I already had the second and third films planned out, but I play hard to get at first because I want them to realize I don't work for them, they work for me.

Back to the Future Part Deux (we're going for class this time) begins where the last one left off. Marty Dotcom and his father George McFly (who has a two year old dependent who won't ever stop crying so the wife is constantly watching him off screen so we don't have to deal with that bullshit) are living happily as billionaires, with Marty owning a mansion in New Zealand with an elaborate safe house in case anyone tries to fuck with them. One day Jim Davis comes by the house to work on the yard because now he's their bitch (bought and paid CASH baby) and he stumbles upon the DeLorean in the garage. He gets in and realizes he can get his revenge on Dotcom by going even FURTHER back in time and starting the whole cat craze before Marty got the chance to. I think you see where we're going with this one. He goes back to the year 1978 and produces a comic strip about a morbidly obese retarded cat named Garfield and he publishes it, becoming the richest man who's ever lived. See, this is the point where it flips to adventure comedy to riveting documentary as this actually happened. We watch Davis's rise to power from lowly time traveler with a good idea to eventual ruler of the planet. Marty and George were able to somehow travel back in time and kick the shit out of Jim Davis and revert what he'd done though they couldn't stop the publication of Garfield which is okay because a totally sweet animated series came out of it.

Once again, I fucking cleaned the house at the Oscars and I rub my Best Picture award on my nuts right in front of Cammy Diaz and tell her to shut the fuck up then I high five Jeff Bridges and tell him to shut the fuck up too and we laugh and become good friends. Universal is ecstatic with the results of my second film for them that they practically beg me to make a third movie, but I tell them I'm creatively drained. They then lobby through congress to make human trafficking legal in America so I can sit in on a Taken style woman auction and they personally bought me each woman (who I spend my days raising on a farm in Pennsylvania) in an effort to get me to do a third film. I reluctantly give in, and I tell congress they can reverse the whole human trafficking thing and I let my women go free (though I occasionally catch them grazing in my yard). What was I talking about again? Oh yeah, Back to the Future Third Strike.

For this one we decided to use the $500,000,000,000 budget on something special. For Third Strike, we actually sent the actors BACK IN TIME to 1985 to interact with the characters of the original film. What better way to close out the greatest time travel trilogy in history then to actually travel through time to film it? The logistics of it don't make much sense, but for five-hundred-billion smackers you can change the laws of physics and logic to MAKE it make sense. And that's exactly what we did. So Marty Dotcom and George "Four Loko Champ" McFly team up with 1985 Marty McFly and 1955 George McFly to fight Biff Tannen and his legion of super bullies. And just for fucking kicks we go to Italy in the mid-70's to create the ultimate Back to the Future/Salo or the 120 Days of Sodom crossover anyone's ever seen. I even prevented the murder of Salo director Pier Paolo Pasolini so that he could go on to make the sequel 2 Salo 2 Serious which was fucking TIGHT. We only did this to give Back to the Future some cred in the art scene, and maybe secure a Blu-Ray release with the Criterion Collection. The scene where Marty Dotcom is forced to eat shit is particularly gruesome, but you can't half-ass art. We actually had Divine come over and take a shit for that scene, we didn't use a Snickers bar like Pasolini had been doing in his movies.

We eventually said our goodbyes and jetted back to the future (CHECK OUT THAT SWEET PUN BRO) and the film opened to the highest opening weekend in the history of cinema. Literally every person, young and old, skipped work and school to come see my movie. Every person who ever existed saw it and loved it and it was given a perfect 10 rating on IMDB and it brought about world peace. The surviving members of The Beatles all fucking died because it was so good. As usual, I showed up at the Academy Awards with a nasty hangover in my pajamas, cursed at the crowd, and took home every award. I then told everyone I thought Lady Gaga was stupid as Hell and everyone asked for a refund for everything they ever bought her which lead to her filing for bankruptcy right there on the spot and then she fucking died which was pretty cool but a little much in my opinion.

I would later become the most hated man on the internet when we released the Back to the Future trilogy on DVD/Blu-Ray/VHS/Beta/Laserdisc/and Hong Kong VCD because I made a brief edit to one scene where a midget in the background killed himself on camera. The edit involved me stopping the movie and zooming in to the midget killing himself and then it cuts to me laughing hysterically for a good thirty minutes and then the movie starts back again where it left off. I really don't know what the big deal is, it was just a tiny artistic edit that I couldn't do at the time the movie originally came out. You can't please anybody these days, you really can't.

Universal Pictures, if you're listening, I'm here and available to do this reboot. You can look at the records and say that it's a big risk to make this move, but look at what I have plans. We're bound to change film making for the better, and there's a lot of money to be made.

WHY I LOVE STAR WARS

Growing up I generally kept to myself and learned what to like from what I saw on TV. As a seven year old I had a few friends who were into Star Wars, but I had never seen it. My dad loved it, but him and my mom were divorced and he lived in New Jersey with my brother, while my mom and I lived in Arizona. My older brother Walter, who I refer to as "brother" and he refers to me as "the boy" (we were big Simpsons fans growing up), got to see the re-releases of the original trilogy with my dad, whereas my mom wasn't so interested in taking me. Because of this, I never really got to experience the original trilogy.

The first time I saw a Star Wars movie was in the Summer of 1999 when my dad took me to see Star Wars Episode I The Phantom Menace after my mom and I moved back to New Jersey. It was awesome, mostly because I got to spend some time with my dad after not seeing him in so long. I pretended to understand what was going on and didn't realize until I was older that the plot didn't make any sense at all to even intelligent people who paid attention to details. I didn't get to see Episode II in theaters, I forget why actually, for some reason I just didn't get to see it. I think it was because that summer my mom and I were preparing for another move, so we just didn't have the time to see it. By this point I still hadn't seen the original trilogy, either.

In April 2005 my brother and his friend Spencer were insanely hyped for Episode III, and I had very little interest because by that point I realized Episode I wasn't that great, so I figured Star Wars wasn't that cool. But of course, being the little brother and wanting to be a part of the group, I faked my hype for it. We watched Episodes I, II, and the original trilogy to work ourselves up for the flick, and the whole time I pretended like I had already seen them all so they wouldn't call me out for not being a fan. It wasn't that I didn't like the films, in fact when we watched them all I became a fan over night, I just didn't want them to think I hadn't seen them before. I was terrified of them discovering my dark secret and then calling me out for being a poser when all I wanted was to hang out with my older brother and his best friend.

The day came when the tickets were finally available for the midnight premiere, and at the time Spencer was working off a debt to me by paying for my lunch every day because I did his homework for him. This day was different, though, as he laid out an offer for me. He said he'd either buy my lunch that day or he'd pay for my ticket to see Star Wars with them at the midnight premiere. At the time I was just a chump 14 year old kid, I didn't know any better, and I was hungry that day! Both my brother and Spencer were skipping lunch that day so they could buy their Star Wars tickets, and I said "fuck Star Wars, I want a double cheeseburger." Spencer then looked at me like I just told him I killed his parents and said "Are you fucking kidding me? You'd give up Star Wars for a cheeseburger?" I know, I know. But you don't really have common sense when you're 14 years old and starving because you were running late to school that day.

Lucky for me, my brother was gracious enough to buy me a ticket, even if he did make me work it off by doing his laundry for the month. Lookin' back I think I got the short end of the stick, but I saw it more as punishment for my dumb decision to choose food over the trilogy. To this day whenever we talk about Episode III they always bring up how I almost gave up Star Wars for a cheeseburger. Not just a cheeseburger, but a double cheeseburger no pickles with onion rings instead of fries and a medium Dr. Pepper mixed with Coke. How do I remember what I ordered that day? Well, we had Burger King every day during the month of May for one reason: Star Wars toys.

Lucasfilm entered a promotional deal with Burger King where every Kids Meal came with one of 36 Star Wars toys. Every week there'd be five different toys to choose from, and the coolest one was the Darth Vader one which only came one per shipment. We ate there every day just to collect the toys, and that itself was an experience to never be forgotten. We'd sit at the same booth every day, we'd order the same thing we'd gotten the day before, and we'd sit around telling jokes until we realized we were running late for 7th period.

One moment in particular I'll never forget was when Spencer told this horrible black joke. "Why can't Stevie Wonder read? Because he's black!" Holy shit, we could not stop laughing, it was the funniest thing we'd ever heard up to that point. It was like the second coming of Carlin to us. It wasn't until the laughter died down that we realized there was a group of big black guys in the booth behind ours that didn't find the joke as amusing. The minute we noticed them glaring at us we grabbed our half eaten burgers and booked it right out the door.

Another humorous moment was when I got the coveted Darth Vader figure. I asked the guy to show me what toys they had that day, they knew the drill, we had been coming every day so they would show us all the toys and we'd pick which ones we wanted. This day was different because instead of taking them out for us the guy just moved his hand around the box, and I saw him toss a toy aside. Knowing damn well what he just did, I totally called him out for it and said "Which toy was that?" He reluctantly pulled it out and passed it to me, and I was amazed, it was the greatest thing in the world. It was a big headed Darth Vader that splits in half revealing an Anakin Skywalker figure inside. It was absolutely wonderful, and it was mine.

I brought it back to the table and showed the guys and they were amazed that I'd had the balls to call the guy out on trying to take it from

Here's a picture of my brother and me at a work buddy's New Year's Eve party. Note my totally sweet Sonic shirt.

me. Finally, little Kris showed some gumption and stood up for himself, even if it was just for a toy that I was 7 years too old to play with. I got up to get ketchup and napkins, and when I got back the toy was gone and Spencer was smiling, eating some of my onion rings, and doing his classic "heeheehee" laugh that he does when he knows he just did something wrong. At this point I was filled with an uncontrollable rage at him, because as much as I'd looked up to him, when I was dating this chick he would constantly tease her for dating me, to the point that she dumped me. He was just goofing around, as Seniors always did to the Freshmen, but she took it to heart. So I exploded on him and went "First you eat my onion rings, then you steal my Star Wars toy, and you HARRASSED MY GIRLFRIEND INTO DUMPING ME!" Oh my God, my brother was crying he was laughing so hard. It only became a problem when I started beating on Spencer, but as a 14 year old kid against an 18 year old, I wasn't doing much damage. We eventually hugged and made up, and he gave me my toy back. Friends shouldn't fight, whether it be over girls or toys or onion rings.

The day was here, I remember it clearly, it was a Thursday and we had all dressed up in our Jedi robes and lightsabers and went to school. A few other kids brought their lightsabers to school, it was a small trend we started for a few weeks building up to the release of the movie. Today was different though, as one kid who brought his to school decided he wanted to have a lightsaber duel with me. It was just a little whacking at each other in the halls, nothing too dangerous, but then this other kid wanted to get involved. Not having a lightsaber, I handed him mine and the two started going at it gently like we were when I was involved. Unfortunately, the newcomer got whacked in the face and didn't take too kindly to it, so he started throwing real punches at the other kid. This was the first actual fight to happen in this school the whole year, and for a school to go from September to May without a single fight is nothing short of miraculous.

I was called into the vice principal's office later that day because it was my group of friends that started the Star Wars trend, and he wanted to know if I had been involved in it to any extent. Lying through my teeth, I explained to him how Star Wars was a big part of everyone's lives and how this incident had nothing to do with me. He asked me why kids were bringing in lightsabers, and I told him it was because this was the last Star Wars film to see release in theaters and it was kind of a special thing to everyone because we all grew up with the films. Being a fan of the originals himself, he told me to junk my lightsaber in my locker and leave it there for the rest of the day. He then sent me on my merry way, and I bolted back to English class.

School got out at 3:00 and my dad took off from work early so he could take pictures of my brother Walter, Spencer, and myself in our costumes. He was immensely jealous he couldn't come with us, at first he thought it was a stupid idea but now he's kicking himself for not getting a ticket. Around 4:00 we got to the theater and saw a big group of our friends at the front of the line. At the time they WERE the line, aside from a few other people, so we got in with them and got comfy because it was gonna be a long wait. How many hours is it between 4:00 PM and 12:00 AM? Enough to drive anyone crazy, lucky for us though, this theater was prepared.

You see, every time a major movie comes out Big Kev from Big Kev's Geek Stuff (also famous for being The Opie and Anthony Show's resident geek) would arrange a huge midnight premiere event at the Clifton Commons AMC in beautiful Clifton, New Jersey. The theater would send people out with snack carts filled with popcorn, candy, and various sodas and ICEEs, and Big Kev would do trivia contests where he'd give out prizes to people who got the answers right. The festivities wouldn't really start until about 6 or 7, so until then we all played the Star Wars games for Nintendo DS, watched the other movies on portable DVD players, or we'd get up and have lightsaber battles. Passing the time wasn't hard, but we were all more excited than words could explain. By the time they let us into the theater at 9 it felt like 3 hours was going to take an eternity.

Big Kev wouldn't take his post at the front of the theater until 10, so we were mostly just sitting in the theater seats talking about whatever until he showed up. At one point my brother and Spencer decided to get up and stage a lightsaber fight at the front of the theater. This was especially awesome because we were the only ones in costume, and they had the VERY expensive Force FX lightsabers. Today you can get those anywhere, but at the time these were only available by calling the number on the commercial that didn't announce the price. The truth was, if you had to ask, you couldn't afford it. These guys poured all their hard earned cash from the weeks prior to afford these lightsabers just for this night, while I had just your standard Toys "R" Us plastic lightsaber. So they went to the front of the theater and began their highly choreographed fight sequence (really, they spent hours in the backyard practicing this), and the crowd was going wild cheering them on and laughing at how goofy it was. Eventually, one of the ushers told them to stop, but said they could do it outside for the people on line. We held onto their seats on line, and they went outside and had a lightsaber battle and then others started joining in. There's a video somewhere on the net specifically of Spencer fighting against a green woman with a blaster (I think she was in the wrong theater).

They came back into the theater and took their seats, and since we were first on line we were in the best theater right in the middle seats of the middle row, so we had the best view in the house. Eventually Big Kev came out and started making jokes about "those two overdressed guys playing make believe" and it was hysterical. He gave out some prizes, and Spencer tried so hard to answer some trivia so he could win, but Big Kev didn't pick him to come down. After all was said and done, Big Kev announced that it was 11:50 and the movie would be starting in ten minutes. He left us to our excitement, and when I tell you that any one of us would've killed for them to start the movie a few minutes early you'd think I was lying. Those ten minutes felt like an eternity, longer than the entire night, longer than the day at school had been, even longer than the whole month between buying our tickets and that minute.

Finally the moment was there, and black screen came up revealing blue lettering saying "A long time ago in a galaxy far, far away..." Someone in the audience actually had the balls to take a picture with a flash disposable camera, which sent the audience into throws of laughter. We were all in nerd heaven, and who could blame us? Our parents got to

I couldn't find any pictures from that night specifically, but here's a picture of me and Spencer at the premiere of The Dark Knight. No, he didn't dress up like the Joker, that's just his normal face.

enjoy the original trilogy, and here we were getting to keep the tradition going with our own trilogy. This was the last film in the Star Wars saga to be released in theaters, and it was ours. Nobody could take that moment away from us. The night was ours.

After the movie was over it was almost a depressing feeling leaving the theater. As a group we all went to the Candlewyck Diner in East Rutherford, which would later become our hangout spot. Here we were, a group of high school kids from Rutherford, New Jersey leaving a movie theater and hanging out at a diner after seeing what would be the most important film of our teenage years. We all sat around the table and laughed and told stories from the weeks before just like a big family, and to be honest it was the first time I was really meeting some of these people. We all went to the same school, but we went with different packs, and Star Wars brought us together. It was an amazing feeling.

After we went home me and my brother had our own brotherly moment in the kitchen, a sort of tradition for us when we lived together. We'd meet up in the kitchen and just chat about whatever over a Coke. I thanked him for pushing me to go with them, and we hugged and went to bed. Well, he went to bed. He didn't have to go to school the next day because it was prom night and the seniors could take the day off to get ready for prom if they needed to. The lucky dog got to sleep in. Unfortunately for me, it was already five in the morning, and I had to be up for school in two hours. Part of the deal of my dad letting me go was that I couldn't bail out of school the next day, I had to honor my responsibilities. Instead of going to sleep, I just played video games for two hours and then went to school. For the most part I was awake the whole day, except for a slight nap in Science class where my friend Danii took my notes for me. She was a great friend, and I'll forever be grateful to her for taking those notes for me. Truth is I never took notes for myself, and I never read the ones she took for me. Sorry, Danii!

That night we made a pact between ourselves that we'd try to make it to every major midnight premiere, and that became our tradition. We saw Batman Begins, The Dark Knight, Iron Man, The Incredible Hulk, Dragonball Evolution, Indiana Jones and the Kingdom of the Crystal

Skull, and a shit ton of other movies I can't remember right now. My dad even came out to see Indiana Jones with us, a move he later regretted and said "I will never see another midnight premiere with you guys." He's since kept that promise. The one thing I will say, though, is that no matter how big the movie and how many people go, nothing will ever top Star Wars. I'm now a lifelong, die-hard fan, not because of the films themselves (as great as they are), but because of the memories we made with them.

CHAPTER 3

THE HIGH SCHOOL YEARS

THE ORIGIN OF KAIL

The summer of 2006 is one I'll probably never forget, mostly due to the fact that it was the first summer where I actively left the house on a regular basis. Every day I'd go over to Pete's house and hang out with him and Teller and their Irish friend Paul who was visiting for the summer. The four of us would spend every day playing video games, going to the mall or the movies, or just walking around town, and it was a blast. We always kept each other in stitches constantly, which eventually lead to the start of my comedy career. This is the origin of Kail.

One day we decided to stay inside and hang out instead of going out, so Teller brought over his PS2 to Pete's house and we set up station in the living room. Teller and I were playing Sonic 2, alternating turns based on deaths of course, and Pete was playing the same game on his laptop. As we're playing, Teller starts singing free-style to the background music in the game. Specifically, we were at the Hill Top Zone level and he began singing from Sonic's point of view how he wanted to have sex with Tails, and how he thought Tails was hot. Naturally, I was in stitches. This was the funniest thing in the world to me, and I'd never seen this done before.

This was two years before Brentalfloss came along and made the "video game music with lyrics" genre what it is, so it was entirely out of left field. I'd begged him to let me record him doing it, and he got stage fright and wouldn't let me.

"You're good with music, why don't you just do it? I'll let you use my lyrics." These would be the words that would seal my fate.

"Alright, I'll do it!"

So I went home that night, opened Sound Recorder (the Windows program that lets you use a computer microphone to record about a minute of sound, the only effects it has is the ability to reverse a recording, yeah that one), and began recording lyrics to the greatest and best song of all time. I was reluctant at first to do Tails is Hot, so I took the music from the Sandopolis Zone from Sonic & Knuckles and I recorded We Got Snakes, which was a song tribute to Snakes on a Plane (which was coming out that month and had been a huge internet phenomenon at the time). I just sat there and sang my little heart out into a crappy 7 year old computer mic, and using Sound Recorder I cleverly lined the tracks up and made an mp3 file of it.

The next day I put it on my iPod and when Pete, Teller, and Paul picked me up I made them hook my iPod up to the stereo. They were laughing hysterically at my terrible singing and ridiculous lyrics, this was suddenly the greatest thing in the world to them. I told them I was going to record an entire album of ridiculous songs and it'd be called "Greatest Snuff Songs Vol. 999," a reference to the HIM album "Greatest Love Songs Vol. 666" that nobody caught. They all said they'd ride my coat tails when I became famous, and right now they're all probably doing much better than I am. That's a boldface lie, me and Teller are about equal, Pete's definitely doing a lot better, and I don't know about Paul, but chances are he's doing pretty good because he went to college and I didn't.

A week after I recorded We Got Snakes I finally recorded Tails is Hot. Again, using sound recorder, but this time I figured out a clever way to do backing vocals too. At the time I didn't know about free software such as Audacity, which might not've even been around at the time, but I didn't care. I felt smart for figuring out tricks of minimalist programs. I even have a history of using Microsoft Paint as my image editing program for as long as I could, only switching to Photoshop when I realized my work looked like shit. After I recorded Tails is Hot I loaded it up onto my iPod and headed out to meet up with the guys.

Another hit right out of the ballpark for the Kail! These guys absolutely ate it up, even though it was Teller's song they thought it was great when I sang it in my own way. Making my friends laugh was the best feeling in the world, but the real treat was having them actually believe I would one day be famous. I tried to come up with more ideas for better songs, but unfortunately I had become a one hit wonder. Those were the only songs I could think of to write.

Eventually the summer would end and Paul would be sent back to Ireland, while we Americans found ourselves going back to school. As soon as I was back in school I started telling my buddy Derek all about my Kail music. He thought it was the greatest thing in the world, and he wanted in on it. I asked him if he wanted to play guitar and we could be a comedy duo, and he accepted such a delightful offer. Thus, Kail and the Bearded Man was born.

Kail and the Bearded Man

Kail and the Bearded Man was a project born out of our desire to play music and be funny. We had the idea to make the music top notch and each show we'd play would follow a storyline about our lives together as best friends. Essentially we were ripping off Tenacious D, though we put our own spin on it, of course, as we'd mixed video game music into our act. The best part was when people would ask us who was who, because at the time we both had pretty prominent beards. In fact, I think mine was thicker and bushier.

Our first show together as a band was in December 2006 when we played a cover of the song Hooray for Santa Claus from Santa Claus Conquers the Martians at the Rutherford High School Holiday Assembly. Every year at the end of the day before Christmas Break started the music department would throw an annual assembly where the choir would sing holiday songs, different students would put on holiday themed skits, and teachers would make jackasses of themselves trying to sing Christmas classics. Every year the principal would come on stage dressed as Santa and he'd pick three students everyone knew (usually a jock, an actor from the drama club, and someone else who was well known) and he'd give them a gift that made fun of whatever they were known for. An example of this would be my older brother Walter: his senior year he performed in My Sister Eileen as the super of the building the main characters lived in (if I remember correctly). One particular scene had him ironing his clothes while standing on stage in boxers and a wife-beater. That year Santa called him to his lap, sat him down, reminded everyone of this scene from the play, made a joke about how those boxers looked worn, and promptly gave him a new pair. They would later stop this practice for numerous reasons: 1.) It was unfair to the kids who didn't get (bargain bag) gifts. 2.) Santa is a symbol of Christianity, so we're treading religious grounds here. 3.) Some might see it as inappropriate that the Principal would openly mock students, even though everyone was okay with it and it was a time honored tradition. They still did the assembly, but they took out Santa without telling anyone, which threw us all into a rage.

Anyhoo, me and Derek told the director of the assembly that we were dying to perform this song Hooray for Santa Claus, and he looked at us like we were morons. He'd never heard of Santa Claus Conquers the Martians before, and maybe he's better off for it, but he gave us the go-ahead after we showed him our act. The day of the show came and we came out on stage with me wearing a Santa hat. Derek started freaking out because he'd lost his guitar pick, and then he yelled at me in front of the whole school for wearing the Santa hat and not telling him so he could prepare too. I calmed him down and took off my hat to reveal a little Christmas present, the contents of which was his beloved guitar pick. He squealed with delight and I said "Yes, Virginia, there is a Santa Claus." We then rocked the house with our thrilling rendition of Hooray for Santa Claus. It was the best first show anyone could ask for, the whole school was laughing and cheering and clapping along to the song.

We'd later found our calling when a new restaurant opened in town: The Blend Café. It was a small café that specialized in these delicious paninis, it was a really low key kinda place. They began doing open mic nights in January 2007, and Derek told me we had to do them. Not being one to go against the direct orders of the guy whose name comes second in the band name, I agreed to partake in such a delightful affair. We practiced a few songs over the course of a few days as we got ready for the big open mic night debut of Kail and the Bearded Man.

January 17th, 2007. That's a day I'll never forget, because it was the day Derek and I got on stage at a small café in Rutherford, New Jersey and made a room full of cool kids burst into laughter. I couldn't tell you what our playlist consisted of for that night, but it was good enough to warrant our coming back to every open mic night The Blend Café did. The second time we went we prepared what would wind up being our most famous song – Ballway to Heaven.

When we rehearsed our songs we always did it in Derek's attic, and 90% of the time spent rehearsing was actually just us sitting around talking about bullshit. In fact, this very day we spent the whole time going on and on about this stupid song by Jim Jones called We Fly High. It was this cheesy hip-hop song that was only famous because a guy yelled out "ballin'!" in the middle of the song. That's why we liked it, anyways. It was so random, at one point the guy in the background yelled out "Grey Poupon!" which, as you should know, is an amazing condiment.

The whole time we rehearsed I just kept singing the lyrics: we fly high, no lie, you know this (BALLIN'!). It was just stuck in my head, for a song so stupid it had a really catchy hook to it. At one point, Derek started Sam Ashing some Stairway to Heaven and I started talk-singing the lyrics to We Fly High over it and it sounded really good, and at the same time was hysterically funny. We could not stop laughing at how stupid it was but how well the lyrics went with the music. This would be our opener at our next big show.

The next time we did the open mic night we started off with Ballway to Heaven and the whole restaurant erupted with laughter. The first open mic night was such a success that the South Bergenite (a local newspaper in Bergen County, NJ) wrote about them, and even contacted me for a quote. I wish I could find the article, but I must've lost it in the move. Basically it was about how the girl who ran the open mic nights set it up and how people like us made it such a success for the restaurant. There were always really talented people coming to these things, but really

Two good lookin' dudes who have the most inappropriate name on the planet, especially in this picture as Kail IS the bearded man.

the audience was mostly made up of kids we knew from high school. That's not a bad thing, considering they kept telling people about it and we always had a good crowd who really dug our stuff. Every time we played we'd open with Ballway to Heaven and everyone who came would sing along and when I yelled out "Ballin'!" they'd all hold their hands up and do the "shoot-the-basket" hand motion, as though they were true ballers like myself. It was a great feeling.

This, unfortunately, wouldn't last forever though. Eventually me and Derek ran out of good ideas for songs, so we just kind of lost interest. He wound up co-founding the band Alex and the Horribles, and they were playing shows and making awesome music. I was still kind of lost with what I wanted to do creatively, so I went on hiatus for a few months.

In May of 2007 I wound up realizing I had potential to do some really awesome things myself, so I came up with the idea to put out free songs on my MySpace page that I'd do for fun in my spare time. Songs like Tails is Hot and We Got Snakes finally got released as I put together the album *Fun and Fancy Free*, which included prank phone calls I'd recorded. Derek and Pete both helped me produce this album, and we'd recorded most of the songs in Pete's living room on one day and the rest in Derek's attic the next day.

Over the next two months my music would blow up on MySpace and I'd received thousands of friend requests. The music was absolutely terrible, it was just me singing over video game music, but people loved it. They thought it was hilarious! At the time Pete was really into photography as a hobby, so we did these really silly photo shoots where he'd follow me around and take pictures of me being really pompous. The pictures had me running around with my long hair, thick beard, and sexy toned arms. Damn, did I look good back then or what?

One of the pictures from the photo shoot we did. I know, I was awesome.

High School Hi-Jinx

Throughout the summer I'd planned to use my time wisely by putting my teenage creative juices to the test. I was planning a VERY low budget movie called Draculo that was going to star Alex from Alex and the Horribles as a typical unemployed slacker named Draculo who's the friendliest guy in town that everybody loves until one day when a new guy moves into town and points out the similarities between Draculo and the vampire Dracula (the similarities begin and end with the name). Realizing Draculo's name is one letter away from being an unholy vampire, the townsfolk go crazy and banish Draculo from the town, and the new guy takes over as king. It was to be my masterpiece, I had an Oscar speech prepared and everything. We filmed a few scenes, and honestly, I didn't prepare any sort of script. Basically our formula was to go out and film Alex doing stupid shit as this character, who was literally just a rip off of The Dude from The Big Lebowski.

We filmed maybe four or five scenes before we gave up on Draculo, mostly because we became very involved in the school play and had no time to film. Yes, it was senior year at good ol' Rutherford High School and me and Alex were actors in The Crucible that year. Senior year me and Alex were inseparable, and the play proved to be no different. I had a main role as old man Giles Corey, and I shit you not my costume was exactly what I wear on a regular basis today: black t-shirt, flannel shirt, and jeans. This play actually sparked my love of flannel, as I hadn't worn it until this cute chick from stage crew let me borrow her shirt for my costume. I had a semi-huge crush on her, and funny enough she looked just like me, sans the horrifying braces, frizzy unkempt hair, and dashing sense of fashion. She let me borrow her flannel shirt (it's cute for girls to wear guy's clothes apparently) and I fell in love. Unfortunately she had a boyfriend, so I had to settle for the shirt, which she didn't let me keep. Bitch.

The director of the play was a round, bald guy with a thick handlebar mustache who looked distressingly like Dr. Robotnik from the Sonic the Hedgehog games. He would always walk in and say "guys how are ya?" Alex fucking LOVED this guy and his catchphrases. Whenever someone would pause during their line he would get up and yell "WHAT IS THIS? A HAROLD PINTER PLAY?!" which was a joke nobody got, so we went to Derek (who had graduated the year before) and we told him what he said and why he'd say it and Derek laughed and pulled out a Harold Pinter script from his collection and showed us. Literally every direction after a line in the play is "Character pauses" or something to that effect. Other catchphrases Robotnik would use included "Guys, we have an audience on Friday" and "we am doomed." The reason why he'd belt out these phrases was because the entire cast would spend the whole time goofing around instead of actually rehearsing. In fact, I'm pretty sure me and Alex spent most of our time under the stage in the "dungeon," which was this creepy basement where they kept all the old props and costumes. We'd go down there and horse around for hours because we always got yelled at for horsing around on stage.

Days before the play was set to open, the cast was nowhere near ready. Nobody had their lines memorized, we were still boxing scenes, and costumes weren't close to being done. Robotnik belted out one final "we am doomed" before proposing the idea of us all having print outs of our scripts taped to different props we'd be using. During the courtroom scene we had papers on our desks, those papers being our scripts, and me having already memorized my lines I just scribbled on them. I wrote things like "shitting dick nipples" and "Robotnik can suck my cock" because I was an awesome rebel teen. I was so awesome that during important scenes in the play I would try to make my fellow actors laugh by ad-libbing lines from Transformers. Specifically, there was a scene where a priest was talking about killing an accused witch or something and his line ends the scene, but me being the dick I am, I went over to him and I go "freedom is the right of all sentient beings, father" and the curtains dropped on that line instead. Luckily the priest was played by fellow comedian Ramy Youssef, so he had a good attitude towards my slip-in. During the final performance in the climactic courthouse scene my character is supposed to attack another character, and during this scene I was supposed to just allow myself to be dragged away by the other characters, instead I threw them off me and looked him in the eyes and said "One shall stand, and one shall fall." During this same scene, Alex wound up getting the papers I had the night before, so he discovered that I had vandalized them with obscenities. He tried with all his might to keep from bursting out with laughter.

During this same time period, Alex and I were in the same theater class. Our teacher hated us, she absolutely had it out for us, and for some reason she loved They Might Be Giants, so I'll call her Ms. Giants. Whenever me and Alex would goof around, she'd always scream at us, and Alex, being the ballbuster he was, would scream right back. He'd do this howl that makes me laugh to this day that sounds like a high pitched "nyeeeeeeeeehhhh!!!!" It was absolutely ridiculous. Whenever we'd be too much to handle, she'd send us down to the "dungeon" to clean the costumes and arrange the props. She knew it, we knew it, everyone knew it – we weren't going to do shit down there but goof around. That's exactly what we did. I remember we opened up a can of paint down there and spilled it all over the floor, but I think that was an accident that we just found pure amusement in more than it was a deliberate attempt at vandalism.

A couple times a month Ms. Giants would call out sick, and the busy work she'd give us would either be to watch a 20 hour documentary series on vaudeville, or to make posters to hang around the school to promote whatever was going on in the theater program at that time. During The Crucible, me and Alex made posters that more or less had something to do with the play. Alex drew the main character yelling "God is DEAD!" during the courtroom scene with Satan coming out of a can of beans (???), and I drew the main character standing on top of a cliff holding a sword to the sky and proclaiming the same thing. Ms. Giants liked them enough to actually hang them up in the hallways of the school, which we thought was hilarious. For the next play, Hello, Dolly, we got to do the same thing, though this time we really pushed it to the next level. Alex drew KISS hanging out with Wayne and Garth from Wayne's World with the title HELLO, DOLLY at the top in hippie style font, and above that in smaller lettering "A Mike Robotnik Joint". For mine I googled the poster for Jurassic Park and redrew that – the dinosaur emblem with the words Hello, Dolly replacing Jurassic Park. I even kept the tagline "a film 200 million years in the making." Needless to say, Ms. Giants wasn't so amused with our work this time around.

Did I fail to mention that I was the lead in Hello, Dolly? Well, I was, and I didn't intend to be. You see, even though I love to sing, I hated doing musicals. I don't know why, I just didn't like the idea of singing in a play. At the time I was more interested in finding a job and working on the next Kail album than I was interested in singing in a play. So I told Robotnik I wasn't going to audition, he took it pretty hard, but he accepted it. A few days later during the auditions he comes to me in the hallways and tells me he needs me for a very specific part, I'd have maybe 6 lines in the whole musical, I wouldn't even have to show up to auditions. My character? A small time artist by the name of Horace Vandergelder. I accepted it without even looking at the script, only because I knew he was serious when he said guys weren't interested in auditioning for the play.

A few days later we're at Derek's house and Derek's congratulating me on getting a major part. I reassured him it wasn't a major part, and pointed out that Robotnik said I only had six lines in the whole play. Derek pulls out his script of Hello, Dolly and points out how my character wasn't just a major character, but the male lead. The only part bigger than mine would be that of the musical's namesake – Dolly. I was absolutely furious. What happened to working on my second album? What happened to getting a job? Those were out of the question now, I'd have to give up any shot at doing either so I could focus 110% on this musical.

For the first few weeks I didn't have to show up to rehearsals because they started production off with the ensemble, but for some reason I came anyways. Oh, alright, it was because of a girl, not just any girl though, this was one I was seriously crushing on. Not my typical "she's cute so I'm going to try to make her my girlfriend so I won't be forever alone," this one had something about her. She was working with the stage crew at the time, and I didn't know who the heck she was. It was so embarrassing because you're supposed to generally know everyone who you're working with, but for some reason I didn't know this chick. I corrected that immediately, though, and I went over to her and started talking real casual like. I asked her what she was up to, she told me she had to take count of everyone who showed up to rehearsal, and from there we would just talk during rehearsals. She'd known me because I was a senior, but I honestly did not know who the hell she was, but then I found out. She was the younger sister of one of my closest friends.

If there's one guideline for every bro to follow on how to live his life it's The Bro Code. For those of you who aren't aware, The Bro Code is a set of rules popularized by Neil Patrick Harris's character on the hit show How I Met Your Mother. It's essentially a list of do's and do not's that every guy should be aware of, it's been passed down from generation to generation and it's basically a guide on how not to step on someone else's toes, and how to conduct yourself so you don't look like a jerkoff in front of women. Things like bros before hoes, never lock eyes with a bro during a devil's three-way, shit like that. Well, unbeknownst to me, I was about to break one of the major rules of The Bro Code: never attempt to get with a bro's sister.

I'm not gonna say who it was, nor will I in any way describe her other than the fact that she was really cute. It never hit me that they were in any way related until she added me on Facebook not long after we started talking, but by then the damage had been done. I was totally digging her, and she was totally digging me too. The unfortunate reality, though, was that her brother knew how I was with women. At the time I was all talk, but his idea of me was that I was this womanizing player. Really, it couldn't be further from the truth, as I'd only totally achieved with two girls up to that point. Maybe three, I don't really remember, but the point is that I really didn't start racking up the numbers until after high school. Lucky for me, he didn't know that this mutual attraction was going on. The most he would ever see was us walking home from rehearsals together, which was easy to play off because we were neighbors and we usually walked home in a group with other people. Really, I felt like this would be a secret I would take with me to my grave, but I figure the statute of limitations is up and it's cool to talk about this now.

Basically our routine was that we'd text every now and then, I'd hang out with her at rehearsal when it was a rehearsal I really wasn't needed for, and then we'd walk home together. Every now and then we'd go to Dunkin Donuts and get those awesome flatbread sandwiches they had. One night in particular that I'll never forget, we were walking home from Dunkin Donuts when she mentioned she wanted to pick up chap-stick from Rite Aid, so on the way home we stopped and she got some. It was blue raspberry flavored, she said it had the most amazing taste she ever had with chap-stick, and she asked me if I wanted to taste it. I looked at her like she was crazy and said "I'm a dude, we don't wear chap-stick." It wasn't until nearly a year later that I realized she was trying to get me to kiss her. On the lips. Man I was such an idiot. An opportunity like that never arose again, not only did I never achieve with her, but I never even got a kiss. Really, I wasn't trying to achieve, I had a huge crush on her and wanted to do romantic things like go for walks in the park and go out on dates and maybe kiss on the lips.

Like I said, we kept it a secret from everyone for basically the whole time it was going on, but now that I was well aware of who she was and who she was related to, I felt compelled to ask for her brother's blessing. I had planned to go up to him like a man and tell him how I felt and ask him if it was cool to totally date his sister. Even though it goes against The Bro Code to date a bro's sister, there can always be exceptions so long as everyone involved is cool with it. In reality, a confrontation like this could've lead to disaster. Right now I was treading dangerous waters, but I was letting sleeping dogs lay. Had I confronted him about it, it could've rocked the boat of friendship and possibly sank the ship if he wasn't cool with it. So of course, I went to Alex about it first.

I told him everything, and he said I should leave it the fuck alone. Alex told me flat out I should stay away from her, and that he was already suspicious of me hanging around with her. He said it was "weird" that I was hanging around his sister. Not wanting to rock the boat any further, I went to her and told her I couldn't keep doing it, and funny enough she told me she was just about to say the same thing. I'd be a complete fucking liar if I told you it was that easy. While we're still friends now, it still makes me wonder what could've happened if things went a little different. Oh well, everything happens for a reason right?

112

KAIL THE SCOUNDREL

In my Class of 2008 yearbook I should have been voted Class Clown, but due to politics I was delegated to Most Unique instead. Why? Because a seriously less funnier than I dude was more well liked. Apparently like Biff Lomen I'm liked, but not well liked. Why do I think I should've gotten Class Clown? Well, basically because of the antics I went on about throughout my entire high school career. I'll take most unique, but the guy who's standard outfit consists of a black CKY shirt and the same ratty old blue jeans every day doesn't exactly come off as "unique."

Aside from my antics in the plays, I was something of an all-around jokester. As you probably already know seeing as you've made it this far in the book, I am a funny dude. I wasn't born with these skills, though, fortunately for me I've had many mentors. One of my favorite mentors is fan-favorite co-host of Destroy All Slackers (my old podcast) – Andrew Teller. He was a grade ahead of me, same class as Derek, Pete, and Sos. He'd previously taught me how to freestyle over video game music, now he'd teach me how to handle a creepy gym teacher.

We had this one gym teacher who was constantly creeping on the helpless girls, let's call him Mr. Jerk. One day Mr. Jerk was looking at this one really hot chick who we'll call Nikki, she was standing alone in the gym waiting for the class to be told what the plan was for the day as the female gym teacher took attendance. Jerk walked up to her nonchalantly and asked her "Hey, Nikki. If you could have any superpower in the world, what would you pick?"

Unaware of his creepy intentions, she responds "Um…. I don't know, maybe flight?"

"Well, I'd pick X-Ray vision!" He says as he gives her a wide-eyed look and looks her up and down.

She doesn't know exactly how to react to this, and lucky for her Teller, Alex, myself, and a few other dudes were five feet away and we saw the whole thing happen. Showing he's got balls bigger than all of us, Teller walked up to Mr. Jerk and looks him in the eye.

"Dude, Mr. Jerk, that's really fucking creepy for a gym teacher to say to a girl." He said laughingly.

Jerk just looked around for a minute before backing away slowly and making believe none of this even happened. We all laughed hysterically and high fived Teller for being so awesome. That moment laid the foundation for how I would act for the rest of my high school career, and most of my adult life for that matter. I seriously did look up to Teller, he was the Qui-Gon Jinn to my Obi-Wan Kenobi. I thought he was the funniest guy in the world, everything he did had me in stitches. The only class we had together was gym, but throughout high school I'd see him in passing through the halls and he always had some funny dance motion or catch phrase to throw at me when he passed.

I would take all these things Teller would do or say and commit them to memory and put my own spin on them. You know how when you hang around your friends long enough you start to act like them and vice-versa? Well, me and Teller really played off each other. In my classes I was constantly yelling out random catchphrases we had come up with, like we were obsessed with this dumb cartoon called Thugaboo. It was this incredibly offensive Wayan's Brothers cartoon pilot they pitched to

Nickelodeon that they actually aired about this group of inner-city kids who each represent a different racial stereotype. We thought it was so hilarious, so we'd walk around the school asking like gangsters, and whenever something was cool to us instead of calling it "dope" or "fly" we'd refer to it as "thugaboo." One thing we'd say is "Yo, dawg, that is THUGABOO." Or we'd say "Thugaboo for LIFE, son!" We'd make gang signs, we had different handshakes, and we'd yell out those silly gang noises. It was absolutely ridiculous.

Teller graduated in 2007, so I had to go through all of Senior Year without him. That's okay, because I had Alex as my partner in crime, and Chris Catoya was our McLovin. Chris Catoya was a character in his own right, we called him the Catman and we constantly knocked him for being smart, but seriously lacking in social skills. We gave him a part in Draculo as Timmy, the idiot boy who couldn't get a date for his life. The only reason we gave him this role was because he actually had a date coming up and we were gonna follow him and film it for the movie just to goof on him.

One thing Chris Catoya was good at was guitar. Now that Derek was busy with college and Alex and the Horribles, Catman thought he could fill the void Derek left in my heart. He always said he could grow a beard and replace Derek as the Bearded Man, and I was always against it, because I knew in my heart that one day Derek would come back to me. I did give him a shot when the 2007 Holiday Assembly came up, though. The week before we'd gone to the movies to see Alvin and the Chipmunks, a decision I will never regret as it was an awesome movie, so I told him we should do a cover of "The Chipmunk Song (Christmas Don't Be Late)," we could get Alex involved, and we'd get a teacher to be Dave. I told him to play guitar for it, which he was down to do, and it was going to be me, Alex, and Ramy singing.

We all met up at Catman's house to practice, and for some reason Catoya couldn't get it right. You see, the song wasn't exactly meant to be played on guitar, it was originally a piano piece with other musical accompaniment. Try as he might to get it to fit, he couldn't rework it as a guitar song, though for some reason Jason Lee was able to play it on guitar in the movie (did Jason Lee actually play it? I don't know, that's irrelevant). At the end of the day we threw Catman out of the act and had the music teacher play it on the piano, and it was great. Alex, Ramy, and myself all sang hilariously bad and we had one of the English teachers play Dave and he got his lines down perfectly. I used to have a recording of it, but for some reason I can't seem to find it. It was amazing though.

Later on in the year, I felt almost kind of bad for leaving the Catman high and dry like that at Christmas. Popcert 2008 was coming up, which was the school's annual talent show where students get together to perform different songs on stage in front of the whole town. I was planning to do Detroit Rock City by KISS, and I wanted Cats to be my Ace Frehley. The teacher running Popcert this year was a huge douche, and instead of just letting everyone who auditioned perform and have fun with it, he cut numerous acts that had good potential and only kept the ones he liked. He didn't like me too much for some reason, be it my pompous attitude, my loud outbursts, or my dashing good looks, for some reason he just did not care for the Kail. Because of this, he'd cut my act the year before, though I still got to play in that one.

Popcert 2007 was kind of a funny trip for me, even though my act was cut, I was still playing bass in another act. I had a huge crush on this girl and I wanted so badly for her to notice me and give me a chance, and when Popcert came around she asked me if I could play bass. Never having touched a bass in my life, I moronically said "Yeah! Anything you need!" She wanted to do White Rabbit by Jefferson Airplane, simple enough, I could learn that in a day. I knew how to play guitar already, so it wouldn't be so bad. I ran to Derek that day and begged him to give me a crash course, and he lovingly embraced my foolish schoolyard romantics. He taught me how to play the song and even let me borrow his bass to practice at home. A week before the show I went out and bought a brand new bass using my last check from Wendy's before I quit. We played the show and it was awesome, and at the end of it she gave me a big hug. That's all I got, and I found myself playing in the Friend Zone Act 1.

Back to 2008, I wanted to do Detroit Rock City, so I had Catman play guitar for me, and we told the teacher setting it up that we were going

Why would I admit this picture exists? Me and Ramy at his 17th birthday party. He looks good, as usual, but I look like a damn fool.

to buy costumes and do it in full make-up. I won't bury the lead, so I'll flat out tell you we lied to him to get him to okay our act. Alex hopped on board, not to play an instrument, but to help with our theatrics. As a goof, we were gonna get a group of the kids who's acts didn't make it in our act as dancers so they could at least be in the show.

Throughout the weeks leading up to the show I'd begun neglecting my responsibilities. I'd repeatedly shown up late, to the point where it became a daily occurrence for me to show up around 9:30. School started at 8, but you could be late as many times as you wanted so long as you were there by 9:30. First period for me was Studio Art, which I'd given up on because I'd lost interest in art and didn't need to pass that class to graduate. Second period for the second half of the year was study hall, and third period was… I honestly don't remember, but it wasn't that important. I'd skip first and second periods and just go to third and that's how I'd start my day, but it eventually got bad as I was coming in super late, sometimes I wouldn't even come in until fifth period, which was gym. If you didn't get the memo earlier in these pages, my gym teacher was Mr. Jerk, and he liked me about as much as I liked him.

The day of Popcert was here and I was ready to put my A game on and put on the best show of my life, unfortunately I'd pulled my "woke up late" card and strolled into gym late. Mr. Jerk calls me out on it with a smile on his face and says "Mr. Kail, I hope you're aware that if you show up for a half day of school on the day of a performance you won't be allowed to attend it." He was right, the school did have a rule against it, but I wasn't much for rules in those days.

"Yeah? Well, it'll be hard to refund all those tickets when the best act in the show isn't allowed to perform. The school will have to answer to 700 angry customers." I said with a smug look on my face.

"Trust me, nobody will be crying if you don't put on your best Gene Simmons impression." Asshole, he didn't even realize Paul Stanley was the singer on Detroit Rock City.

Since I was late he made me run laps the whole period, good thing I walked to school every day because I was in good enough shape to do those laps. Had it been me today I'd be passed the fuck out after two laps.

At the end of the day I went home and got ready, I was planning on sneaking into the show anyways, what did I care about the rules? Worst that would happen is they tell me I can't perform, but I had to try.

My act was the one before the last, it would've been the closer but the director liked the student who did close. I didn't mind, as he was a good musician, but being the egotistical jerk I was I knew it wasn't because of his talent that he got there. The whole time backstage the director kept bothering me asking when we were gonna put our make up on, and as a goof I kept telling him "during the song before ours, since some of our guys are playing in other songs." He believed it, and then he had a light heart attack when he not only saw us go on stage without make up, but a crew of others who weren't even in the show coming out on stage in ridiculous costumes me and Alex pulled out from the dungeon.

Before we started performing, I took to the mic and gave a quick speech. As a way of getting myself out of trouble for showing up to the performance when I came to school late that day, I decided to dedicate my act to the vice principal, who'd been in the hospital for a tumor.

"I've spent four awesome years at RHS, and throughout my stay I've caused more trouble than I'd like to admit to. Every time I sat in his office, Mr. Cassidy would give me a different lecture and a different life story that he thought I'd learn from. This song's dedicated to Mr. Cassidy, let's hope he has a speedy recovery!"

We then proceeded to rock the house more than anyone else ever thought we would. During the double solo me and Catman faced each other and I totally went in to open mouth kiss him in front of the whole school. He laughingly pulled away without missing a beat. It was by far the best stage performance I'd ever given.

After the show was over all the parents and friends of performers waited outside the auditorium to say congratulations to everyone who performed. While looking for my people I ran into Mr. Jerk and we locked eyes for a second.

"You put on a good show, Kail, I gotta hand it to you." He said with a smug laugh.

"I told you I'd play, one way or another."

We shook hands and went our separate ways, as much as we hated each other throughout high school and the short time I had him in elementary school, there was a mutual respect between us. Except for the whole he was creepy and always sexually harassed the mildly attractive girls.

Believe it or not, I actually earned enough credits to graduate in June. When I walked across the stage to accept my diploma I attempted to moonwalk so poorly that it came off as hilarious. After graduation, I went on to work at Blockbuster where I learned all about the wonders of retail. I can openly admit that I miss my time at Blockbuster more than I do high school.

CHAPTER 4

BLOGS - PART 2

How GameStop Tried to Sell Me an Open Game as New

If you've ever shopped at GameStop then this has probably happened to you: you walk in, grab a new game off the shelf, and you bring it to the counter to find that the associate behind the counter opens that case and puts a disc in it and tries to sell it to you at full price. They do it to everyone, and last night they pulled that shit on me without me noticing.

I went into GameStop yesterday with a couple older games I didn't play any more with the idea that I could trade them in and make enough to get something new. I'd heard about Hyperdimension Neptunia and how it's a cool JRPG throw-back to SEGA's history, so I figured why not check it out? GameStop had one copy left priced at $29.99 and the label clearly said it was new, so I brought it up to the counter and pulled out my PowerUp Rewards card that contained the $46 I'd made off those trade-ins. He took the case and turned around, threw my copy in the bag, and charged me the $30. I walked out with the bag in hand and headed home.

I got home and saw that they'd given me an open copy of it, but still charged me the full price for it. Pre-Owned it cost only $26, so I wouldn't have saved much money, but still. I knew they did this shit, but they're supposed to ask you beforehand if you still want the game. This guy just threw the copy in the bag sneakily without telling me I was getting an open game. After having spent the entire day running errands, I decided I didn't care and just threw the game into the PlayStation and called it a day. After about fifteen minutes, though, I realized I'd bought what could be considered the worst game of all time. The story seemed really funny, but the character's voices were really annoying, and the first fifteen minutes has you reading dialogue while cardboard cutouts stand next to each other. This isn't 1995 anymore, you can actually put some effort into your games now y'know.

Now I was pissed, the game wasn't anything I thought it was and there was no way I could bring it back because it was opened. I then realized that if I had noticed I'd grabbed the wrong game BEFORE I put the game in the system, I'd still be unable to bring it back. How do I prove I didn't open it if it's already open? Frustrated, I called the store to see if I could at least bring it back for store credit considering it hadn't even been an hour since I'd left the store.

"Thank you for calling GameStop, how can I help you?" The clerk answered semi-pleasantly.

"Yeah, hi, I was just in your store an hour ago. I picked up a copy of Hyperdimension Neptunia and it's not the game I thought it was, I understand I can't get a cash refund but is there any way I can get like store credit or anything? By the way, the game was open when I bought it even though the sticker said new..."

"Did whoever sold it to you tell you it was open?" He asked me, trying to cover the ass of his co-worker who had sold me the game.

"No, he just kinda threw it in the bag and didn't say a word to me about it." At this point the manager would take the phone.

"Hey this is the manager, what was the problem you had?" He asked me.

"Yeah, I just bought Hyperdimension Neptunia, and it really isn't the game I thought it was, and I was charged full price even though it was opened. I just want to bring it back and exchange it for something else if I can." I was being very calm and very polite about it, but I was frustrated.

"Sorry, we can't take it back. You can trade it in for store credit, but you won't get much. If I give you a refund then that means I have to sell it to someone else as new when it's been in your system."

"Dude, not for nothing, but I know a ton of people who currently work and have worked for GameStop. I'm well aware of how you guys open the games and let your employees take them home and play them. I'm not saying your store does it, but it does happen and it's bullshit."

I was pissed now, because it's true. Depending on what store you stroll into, some stores will actually let their employees open new games, take them home, and play them. They do this to make sure the employees know what they're talking about and can suggest games for customers. The general rule of thumb is that you can take out pre-owned games, so long as you return them within a set number of days and you bring it back in the exact condition you took it home in, not that they check. Depending on how many of a specific game come in you're supposed to gut either one copy or a few so it looks like you have a lot in stock. Something like Hyperdimension Neptunia would only get one copy gutted, but any Call of Duty game would have like five to ten copies gutted with those cases on the shelf. I knew one store that was so bad that they would gut every copy of a niche game like Neptunia just so the employees could all take copies home and play them.

The manager said he would give me the full refund as store credit as a personal favor. Gee, thanks. I went over to the GameStop with the game and receipt in hand, walked in, handed him the stuff, and he began the process. He opened the case to check that the disc and everything was still in there and that the disc hadn't been scratched, and what do you know, he fumbled and dropped the disc on the counter where it flip-flopped all over the keyboard of the register computer. Now he has to sell that disc as new to some poor customer. I then walked out of the store with a new, unopened copy of Twisted Metal, after dealing with some of the worst customer service I've seen in years.

Some of you guys might say I'm complaining, but this is a huge problem. Why is it that it's okay for GameStop to sell me an unopened copy of a new game, but my friend who comes later in the day has to take home a copy that someone opened? Sure, maybe they didn't play it, but who knows who touched that disc. The clerk might've been sick, he might've sneezed on his hand and just put the game in the case. Chances are you won't get sick and die, but if I'm gonna risk catching some nerd's disease I at least want a couple bucks knocked off the price.

At least I got a trophy in Neptunia for starting the game before I brought it back.

The List of Achievements to Boost Your Player Score

Often times while sitting alone in my study working on attaining my next Nobel peace prize I will ponder quietly to myself "how did I get to be so great?" There has to be a system set in place to calculate how awesome I am, and retrace my steps to getting to be that awesome. Well, the video games industry solved this problem with the introduction of "achievements," which are tasks you perform in-game that award you with a set amount of points that go to a universal "gamerscore". I decided it was time for there to be a list of sexual achievements that'll help calculate your "player score"

Here are the rules: aside from the first achievement and a few others (namely the milestone achievements), you can count individual achievements multiple times to your score. The reason for this? I'm not going to write up a new sheet of achievements for every girl you score with. So unlike video games, you can do the same thing twice and count it, but NOT in the same sitting. You can go for multiple achievements during one encounter, but you can't do the same thing twice and think it counts to your player score.

Welcome to the Game - 10P - You just had sex for the first time, congratulations!

Sexhaver - 5P - Have sex with someone.

Five in the Bag - 10P - Successfully score with five different people.

Ten in the Bag - 20P - Successfully score with ten different people.

You're Gonna Get Fired - 15P - Score with a co-worker of the same rank or lower than you on the totem pole.

Promotion! - 25P - Score with a superior or higher-up, hopefully this'll lead to a raise, promotion, or a winning lawsuit on your behalf.

Livin' like Kail - 20P - Get someone to come home with you and do it on a blanket of your favorite childhood cartoon character.

For Her Pleasure - 50P - Make a female successfully climax

For His Pleasure - 5P - Make a male successfully climax. Or just be there I guess.

The Devil's Threeway - 15P - You and a buddy tag-teamed some lucky individual, hope you didn't lock eyes!

Eiffel Tower - 5P - You and your buddy high-fived during a Devil's Threeway!

Drake the Explorer - 25P - You did something you probably shouldn't be doing with someone who doesn't belong to the gender you fancy.

The Holy Trinity - 50P - You were the object of affection in a threeway involving two people of the gender you fancy.

Twenty Five Large - 50P - Successfully bang twenty-five different people.

Louis C.K. - 30P - Make your partner laugh during sex without it being at your expense.

Exit Only - 15P - Get your partner to let you slide it in the backdoor.

Screamin' Creamin' - 5P - Five extra points if they scream when it's in the backdoor. Obviously they didn't know what they were getting themselves into.

Hey Jealousy - 15P - Show up at somewhere you know your ex would be and show off your new eye candy in front of them. Extra credit (uncredited) if they text you something catty later that night.

The Love of My Life - 35P - Successfully land that one person you've had a crush on for forever. You know the one I'm talking about. Don't play dumb, we all have one.

Whoops! - 25P - Rebound after accidentally calling your partner by the wrong name.

Good Boy - 25P - Get it on with an older lady. She has to have at least been a legal adult the day you were born for it to count.

The Mother Load - 50P - Totally achieve a holy trinity with two lusty MILFs.

Final Fantasy - 15P - Fantasize about someone you shouldn't be fantasizing about while you're with someone very attractive.

Slamdunk! - 45P - With your buddy's permission, close the deal on a lead he was unable to close with.

Always Be Closing - 50P - Successfully score three gurlz in a row without getting rejected once.

Fifty/Fifty - 250P - Score with fifty different people, better get yourself tested!

There are a total of 865P to earn, but because you can do things multiple times you can calculate yourself an even higher player score. If you got it in you, tally up a score and either tweet it to me (@DudeGurlz), or comment on this post with your score. Maybe I'll eventually reveal my own awesome score. Someday.

How I dress right before I calculate my score every week. No, I'm not sucking in my gut, I'm just that sexy.

I'D LEAVE A JOB OR A WOMAN TO SEE A MOVIE

I love movies, I don't care what anyone says, I'm a movie buff. I love comedies, action/adventures, sci-fi, sometimes dramas, documentaries, classics, anything (except rap or country). Let's face facts, movies are a big part of my life. That's why I'm not above leaving a responsibility or a commitment to see one.

When I was 17 I had a job working at Wendy's as the grill boy. I was the neighborhood chef, always cookin' them patties, and I did it good too! I did a good job, enjoyed what I did, loved getting discounted food, it was a pretty good gig. In April of 2007, though, I wound up butting heads with the managers at Wendy's.

You see, as a lover of cinema I'm required to always be the first to see movies by directors I love, and I love both Robert Rodriguez and Quentin Tarantino. Lucky for me, the two of them worked on a double-feature project called Grindhouse that featured a movie by Rodriguez (Planet Terror) and a movie by Tarantino (Death Proof). In between the movies were a slew of trailers from Rob Zombie, Edgar Wright, and Eli Roth, all directors I enjoyed. It was a cream dream come true, how could I miss this? Unfortunately, I was scheduled to work the whole opening weekend.

I asked my managers for the Friday off, so I could see the movie with my friends at night, but they wouldn't budge. They told me I had to be there the whole weekend, they wouldn't even work with me. What was I supposed to do? I needed to see this movie, and I was beginning to hate the job. Add in the fact that I was in high school and had a lot of work to do, I was in a band, and I was still chasing girls. Working a job that wouldn't work with me wasn't exactly a top priority.

So the Friday that Grindhouse came out, I told my boss I was quitting. They asked me to reconsider and told me they needed me, and I told them if I couldn't get a single day off then why did it matter? It didn't really. So I told them peace out, and moseyed on my way to the picture show. It was one of the best theatrical experiences I ever had.

Fast forward three years later, I'm dating a girl who hates when I hang out with my friends. She absolutely ABHORS it. One thing she hated more than when I wanted to hang out with my friends is when I wanted to go to the movies. She absolutely ABHORRED going to the movies. At this point Iron Man 2 was about to come out, and I was fucking stoked to see it. I loved the first Iron Man, so of course I wasn't about to miss the second.

Right before the movie came out we got into a huge fight over it because I told her I was going to go with my friends to see it, which she didn't take too kindly to. This girl also enjoyed physical altercations (i.e. she used to beat me silly, and that shit hurt), so needless to say this was coming up anyways. She told me she didn't want me to go to the movies, and I stood up for what I believed in and I told her to go fuck herself and that I was gonna see Tony Stark suit up. I had a mean case of Robert Downey Syndrome and I wasn't about to miss out on a sequel to one of my favorite super hero movies. So I broke up with her to see Iron Man 2, which wound up not being that great.

I'm not the only guy who'll break up with his girl to see a movie though, this dude I used to be good friends with in high school did just that so he could come with me to see Dragonball Evolution. Yes. A chap actually dumped his only source of blowjobs so he could come with me to see a terrible adaptation of the greatest action cartoon ever made. They got into a huge fight over, you guessed it, the fact that he was hanging out with his friends. She was so crazy, in an effort to get him back she actually told her parents he was taking her to prom. This didn't work, and he told her parents he was not, in fact, going to prom with her.

Are there any upcoming movies worth leaving my current girlfriend for? I don't know, frankly speaking The Avengers doesn't look all that great. It's a cool concept, but not dump-worthy. It could be the best superhero movie of all time, but based on what I seen it wouldn't be worth the risk with the gal I'm currently with, she's a total keeper. Now The Dark Knight Rises, on the other hand, looks to be the greatest and best film of all time, so I can see myself leaving the entire planet just to see it. Sorry, everybody, but I'm a man who loves his Batman. Lucky for me, my girlfriend loves going to the movies and I'm off on Fridays, so I don't have to worry about leaving anything to see Batman.

These are the guys I leave women and jobs to see movies with – Alex, Sean, and Ramy. Who's the beautiful chap with the long flowing red hair?

THE LOST ANIMATED MASTERPIECE ROCK & RULE

Nelvana's a Canadian animation studio most people remember for the Star Wars cartoons from the 80's, and they're probably most famously remembered for introducing Boba Fett to the world in the animated short featured in the infamous Star Wars Holiday Special. Other than that, you'll probably recall a series of less than stellar pre-teen toons like 6Teen and Total Drama Island, or maybe the Care Bears. The one thing you won't remember Nelvana doing, though, is probably one of the greatest animated films of all time: Rock & Rule.

Rock & Rule is the story of Omar, Angel, Dizzy, and Stretch, a group of friends who are in a band together trying to make it big in Ohmtown. One day a legendary rock star named Mok comes to Ohmtown looking for a "very special voice" to help him raise a demon during his act and he discovers Angel and kidnaps her. Omar, Dizzy, and Stretch then go on an adventure to Nuke York to try and rescue her and stop Mok's nefarious plans. It was the first theatrically released animated film to use CGI, as well as aim for an older teenage audience while still being accessible to children. There are many references to drugs, sex, and Satan worship, but at the same time there's tons of slapstick humor and cute animals to keep kids entertained. Unfortunately this formula wouldn't work and Rock & Rule proved to be a commercial failure.

It came at a time when Nelvana was exclusively working on commercial animation and animated half-hour specials. It was the first successful Canadian animation studio and they wanted to break new ground and make the first successful Canadian animated feature film. Director Clive A. Smith and his rag-tag group of animator cronies began to work on a project called Drats!, which was aimed at a much younger audience, as evidenced by concept art showing off cuter humanoid animals. As they worked on the project it began to shape itself into what would eventually become the darker and more mature Rock & Rule. Work on the film started in 1979 and wouldn't be completed until 1983.

The release of Rock & Rule was riddled with political drama, as it was originally to be distributed by MGM on a scale comparable to any Disney film or Don Bluth film of the time. Contracts were signed, agreements were made, and hands were shook, but unfortunately while the film was still being produced there was some changes made in management at MGM. The heads of MGM who originally loved Rock & Rule suddenly disappeared and were replaced by new heads who didn't understand the picture, and they worked through loopholes in the contract to get the film's release shortened to a small stint in Boston and New York in theaters close to the local colleges. This was done in an effort to attract the "college stoner" crowd, which had made re-releases of Fantasia and other Disney films, as well as Ralph Bakshi's Fritz the Cat and the sci-fi epic Heavy Metal successful animated films. Even after the producers themselves attempted to get asses in seats at these limited showings by driving around in cars littered with Ring of Power decals (as MGM ordered a name change as well as a replacement for the voice of Omar from Gregory Salata to Paul Le Mat), the film proved to be an unsuccessful venture, one that almost closed Nelvana down for good.

Throughout the 80's Canada's own CBC would show the film repeatedly in both an uncut version as well as an alternate cut that contained the original voice actor for Omar, and the film would see release on LaserDisc in Japan (with Japanese subtitles), as well as a hard-to-find VHS and LaserDisc in North America. Eventually the film would find its audience through late-night showings alongside Heavy Metal on HBO, Cinemax, Showtime, and other premium cable networks. As these began to slow down, there began a small, but devoted group of people on the internet calling attention to the film, many of these fans having seen the film on HBO or even the CBC as children.

In 2005 the prayers of the fans have been answered, as Unearthed Studios revealed their intent to release a special edition 2-Disc set of Rock & Rule on DVD. The head of Unearthed Films even kept the internet fans updated on progress as it was made. Being a fan himself, he knew he had to do justice to the film by properly, so he made it a goal to find as much supplemental features as humanly possible that would be interesting to see. The Special Edition set was released in 2006 with director commentary, a making of featurette, the CBC alternate cut of the film, and The Devil and Daniel Mouse, which was one of the specials they did that was the basis for what would become Rock & Rule.

The unique thing about the film, though, wouldn't be in the animation. The soundtrack for the film was comprised of original tracks from Debbie Harry, Cheap Trick, Iggy Pop, Lou Reed, and Earth Wind and Fire, including a mash up between Cheap Trick and Debbie Harry where members of both groups played together and Debbie Harry sang alongside Cheap Trick lead singer Robin Zander. A soundtrack album was planned, but because of the financial failure of the film it was scrapped and most of the tracks went into obscurity. Some of the songs wound up as B-sides on singles released in foreign countries, bonus tracks on albums, or rarities in compilations. A few of the songs would never be released such as the end duet "Send Love Through." Unearthed Films attempted to make the 2-Disc Special Edition a 3-Disc affair, with the third disc being a soundtrack CD, but they ultimately couldn't secure the rights to release the songs on CD.

I consider Rock & Rule to be my favorite film of all time because of the story behind the making of the movie, as well as the actual movie itself being a completely original concept that doesn't talk down to kids and incorporates rock music by popular musicians in an engaging way. DreamWorks animated movies will often use contemporary songs by known bands and artists as a way to try to "relate" to the audience, but more often than not it just doesn't fit the world in which the story takes place. Rock & Rule went above and beyond that and actually got the contemporary musicians to create songs for the characters.

The film itself influenced my unproduced animated film project Destroy All Slackers in a huge way. You could even say I ripped off the plot, but not really. I was heavily influenced by the film and liked the idea of one member of a band leaving the group to go solo and gain success and the rest of the band being annoyed not because of the band, but because of their friendship. This wasn't the plot of Rock & Rule, as it turned out that Angel was kidnapped against her will, but this laid out the idea of the plot in Destroy All Slackers. Even the character of Mok Rockfield, one of the radio hosts that narrate the movie, was named after a character from Rock & Rule.

Really, you're doing yourself an injustice by not checking this movie out. I recently showed it to my girlfriend Katie who absolutely loved it and questioned why it wasn't better known. It was at that moment that it hit me; this truly remarkable animated film isn't well known because nobody talks about it. It's a great flick, and it needs to be mentioned when anyone starts talking about animation. Genndy Tartakovsky referenced it in his Star Wars: Clone Wars cartoon by giving the residents of the planet Nelvaan (which was named after Nelvana) a look reminiscent of the characters from Rock & Rule. Other than that and a Marvel Comics adaptation coinciding with the release of the film, nobody ever really spoke about the film. It was mentioned in a few books, but the general populace is completely unaware of what could be the single greatest animated film ever.

My Sweet Ass Sonic Tattoo

The coolest thing I ever did was get a tattoo of my favorite video game character, Sonic the Hedgehog, on the 20th anniversary of his first appearance. June 23rd 2011 will forever be remembered as the day Kristen Kail abandoned all hope of a normal life. How did it all go down you ask? Well, take a seat and I'll impart what I hope could be some wisdom upon you.

It all started back in April 2011 at the height of Destroy All Slackers mania. Me, Teller, and Sos had been the kings of nerd podcasting, not really, we were just really funny and had a good fan base, but it was great. Every Wednesday we'd get together and sit in my bedroom and shoot the shit about whatever we wanted. By this point if you don't know about Destroy All Slackers then you better go buy my book Slacker's Paradise and read up on ya history, y'all. Anyhoo, it was Spring Break season and I don't remember if it was on the air or off the air, but me and Teller got into a conversation about video game tattoos. Thinking about it, we might've been talking on the air because he started bragging about his pretty sweet Mortal Kombat tattoo he had on his back.

It got me thinking about how I had been a legal adult for two years now, and didn't even have a single tattoo yet.

Now don't go thinking that you have to have a tattoo to validate yourself, because that's not true in the slightest. To me though? Oh, I believed it wholeheartedly. I thought the best way to validate myself as a grown-up and seem cool in front of everyone was if I got a really sweet tattoo. My original idea was to get Donkey Kong on my leg, now that was an awesome design. It was Donkey Kong riding a motorcycle with sunglasses on and they're kind of coming down so you can see he's winking and he's holding a barrel with bananas flying out of it. My friend Hiten did the design for me, he's gotta be one of the best artists I know. I gave him the box-art from DK King of Swing as inspiration and to show him the style I wanted, the next day he gave me exactly what I envisioned.

So I went to a guy I knew to ask how much it would cost and how long it'd take, he said it'd be about $300 depending on who you go to and considering the detail that would go into it. I began to rethink this comedic tattoo I was planning, and then I thought about the fact that the twentieth anniversary of my favorite speedy blue hedgehog was coming up, so I figured "Why not get a Sonic tattoo?" And thus the planning began.

I wrote this whole bit that would make getting the Sonic tattoo worth it. One of my favorite movies of all time has always been American History X, and I especially love the scene where they're having a family dinner and the mom's Jewish boyfriend is talking about the Rodney King case and Edward Norton gets up and yells at him and goes "You think I'm gonna sit back and watch as you POISON my family's dinner with your Jewish, nigger loving bullshit?" and he rips his shirt and points to this huge Swastika tattoo over his heart and he goes "You see this? It means NOT. WELCOME." To me that was one of the most powerful scenes in cinema history, most certainly one of my personal favorites.

The bit I wrote had me with and a bunch of guys having dinner and one of them starts talking up Nintendo and how great their games are. They'd go on and on about how Nintendo has such a lush, colorful history and how their games are timeless masterpieces and what not, and I just wouldn't put up with it. Being a diehard SEGA fan, such talk about

Nintendo offends me to no end. So I get up and yell at the dude and say "You think I'm gonna sit back and watch as you POISON my family's dinner with your Hyrulian, Nintendo loving bullshit? Not on my watch!" and I rip my shirt and point to my Sonic tattoo and go "You see this? It means NOT. WELCOME." It was a hilarious bit that I couldn't wait to rinse and repeat around anyone who talked about Nintendo to me.

By the time I'd settled on the design, which would be the silhouette of Sonic's face as seen in the Sonic Team logo, it'd be mid-June already. At this point I was seriously considering getting the tattoo, it had gone from sort-of joke to actual planning. I remember pulling out my phone and showing one of my work buddies the design and him going "you're fucking crazy, dude." Was I crazy? Probably. Another factor pushing me to get this tattoo was the fact that I was seeing this chick Katie at the time. She was the first girl I'd gone out with in almost a year that I actually wanted to impress, it was really weird for me to date a girl and be so into her that I actually go out of my way to try and look good. I'd been with dozens of girls during the period between Felicia breaking my heart and meeting Katie, and each one I didn't feel like I had to do anything special to impress, but Katie? She was something special. I felt like I had to come off as Dr. Cool Guy in order to get her to stick around, but unaware to me I had already achieved PhD status in the field of absolute chillness. Either way, I figured getting this tattoo would seal the deal in how cool she thought I was. It wasn't the driving force to me getting it, because I did really want it, I guess it was more the last bit of courage that pushed me to do it.

So June 23rd was here and I knew I was going to get it. Me and Teller did a special edition of Destroy All Slackers to celebrate Sonic's 20th Anniversary and in it we talked about how I'd be getting the tattoo that night, and right after we wrapped up the show I went to pick up Katie so we could get me this tattoo. Me and Katie met up with Teller and Sos at the tattoo parlor and I'd brought my Flip Cam so we could film it. The minute we walked in I was led to the back where I'd get the face of my childhood hero forever imprinted on my chest. It was funny because the guy who did it looked EXACTLY like Ryan Dunn, sounded just like him too, and this was literally a day or two after he died. He laid me down on the table and laughed and said "I haven't seen Sonic the Hedgehog since the 90's, do they still make Sonic games?" and I replied with "I don't wanna talk about it, let's just let you keep the memories you have with him untarnished." I didn't want to tell him that Sonic had begun making out hardcore with human princesses and ruin whatever potential memories he had.

Everyone always says that getting tattoos is easy, or that it hurts like Hell, and the truth is it really isn't that bad. I mean, it hurt like a bitch in some spots, felt really hot, a few pinches here and there, but it was over in 20 minutes and after I just felt dizzy. The real pain in the balls, though, was the healing process. That's what people don't tell you about when they tell you about getting tattoos. Every day you have to rub a certain kind of lotion on it and keep it moist, and whatever article of clothing you wear over it is going to be ruined. I bought a pack of wife-beaters and spent a week wearing them every day, not to show off the tattoo, but to not ruin any of my regular shirts. Every day I was wearing a wife-beater with a zip-up hoodie over it, let me tell you how awkward it was going to my niece's middle-school graduation dinner looking like that. Needless to say I had some questions to answer from my grandma.

One thing people always ask me is if I regret getting it, and people often assume I'm going to regret it when I'm 70 years old. Truth is, I was worried about regretting it at first, but after 6 months I've actually forgotten that it's there. Even at home, where I'm usually walking around shirtless if it's a warm day, I barely notice it. Every now and then I'll take a look at it and remember why I got it and it makes me really happy. I got it at a time when my life was Destroy All Slackers, when every day I'd look forward to Teller and Sos coming over on Wednesday to drink some beers and talk about video games and disgusting girls I've hooked up with. I didn't have a care in the world back then, I would just hang out with my bros and kick it old style. In 50 years when I look at that tattoo that's exactly what I'm going to think about, a time when I had fun just talking with my friends and doing an online radio show.

If you're going to go out and get a tattoo, there's no better reason to get one than to commemorate some awesome time in your life. Something that every time you look at it you'll say "hey, when I got this tattoo it helped me get laid" or something cool like that. Cool guys always get laid, remember that, and to be cool you gotta have a ton of sweet memories. If you get a tattoo just because you like the way it looks, you might wind up changing your mind twenty minutes after you get it, but if you get a tattoo that reminds you of something or someone, it'll be fresh as Hell the rest of your life. Well, if you get a tattoo for someone that isn't dead you run the risk of them becoming an asshole at some point and completely ruining your tattoo. The only situation in which I would recommend you get a tattoo for someone is if they're dead, because then they can't become an asshole and ruin your left arm.

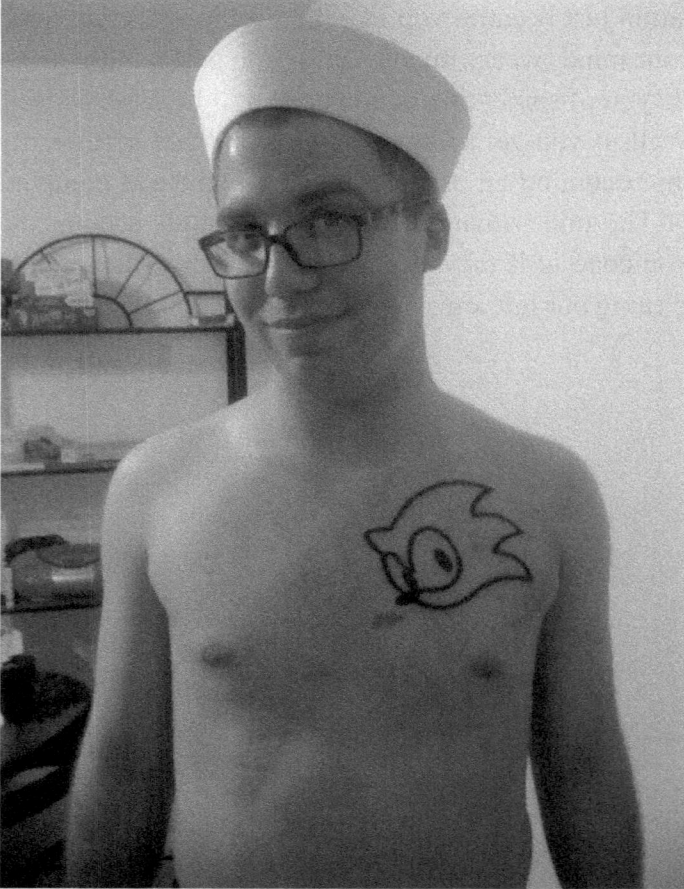

"You see THIS? It means NOT. WELCOME."

Mega Man Universe

Back in 2010 I was working as a budding gaming journalist for a gaming site that will go unnamed (for various reasons), and I got to go to the New York Comic Con to do some field reporting. At the time I was a huge Capcom fanatic, so my first stop was at the Capcom booth.

Capcom had announced Mega Man Universe prior to its appearance at the New York Comic Con through a stop motion animated trailer that didn't really explain much. It showed a kid sleeping, and then out of nowhere his Mega Man toys started running around shooting at various enemies. For some reason, Ryu from Street Fighter makes an appearance. Arthur from Ghosts n' Goblins is there too, for some reason. And the trailer closes with a funny shot of Bad Box Art Mega Man (who's become a character in his own right by this point) just being silly. It was interesting, to say the least, but it didn't show us what the game was really about. Was it a classic style Mega Man game? Was it a Mega Man cross-over brawler? What the Heck was it?

It wound up being a Little Big Planet clone. There was more to it than that, but once they began showing off gameplay clips it became pretty obvious that it had some Little Big influences. It was a classic style Mega Man game based on Mega Man 2 that featured 3D graphics on a 2D plane, except now you could customize your character and customize your levels. You could even upload your creations to the internet for all to see! It was a neat little concept that was meant to be an awesome downloadable game for PSN/XBLA.

When I saw it at the New York Comic Con it was in a very playable state, in fact, they could've released what they had at the NYCC and it would've been good. There weren't many lines for the game, despite Capcom dedicating an entire side of their colossal booth to it, because it was being upstaged by a game on the other side of the booth known as Marvel vs. Capcom 3. Pffffttt. Like that game would ever take off. Amateurs.

Anyhoo, some of the Capcom Unity guys were there showing off Mega Man Universe to the five of us who were interested, and they explained just how the different features worked. You could pick your character (Mega Man, Rock Man, and Bad Box Art Mega Man were on display), create a custom character from various available body parts like some kind of Frankenstein creature, and you could build your levels from scratch or customize existing levels. If you didn't want to do anything like that, you could just pick a character and play a classic style Mega Man game. I got to take it for a ride, and it was pretty cool. Because there were others waiting around to play it, I didn't get to see much of the customization features, but it felt like an actual classic Mega Man game. Each character had different abilities, and it was awesome to see how the Capcom devs specialized the level just for the NYCC. There was an area of the level where the blocks spelled out NYCC 2010, which I thought was a cool little shout out.

That Sunday was the announcement that shook the internet. I stood on line for an hour for the World of Capcom panel where they would be giving updates on various games coming out, and they made a few announcements. Keiji Inafune, creator of Mega Man, was there and he sat down at his spot at the panel table and said "We have a special surprise for all of you." The lights then went dark and a video came up on the screen that showed other conventions where Inafune asked fans what game they wanted to see made the most, and unanimously they all shouted "MEGA MAN LEGENDS 3" to which he responded simply with "Thank you." The video then went on to show the logo for Mega Man Legends 3 Project. The rest of the panel was spent exclusively talking about how they wanted the fans to be involved with the production of Mega Man Legends 3, and then they showed some VERY work-in-progress concept art. It was one of the coolest panels I'd ever been to, the first where such a legendary announcement was made. I was in nerd heaven.

Then both games were cancelled.

Before the announcement of the cancellation of both games, Keiji Inafune announced he was leaving Capcom. There was speculation that because the head honcho for both projects was no longer working on the projects that both would be junked in favor of Capcom's more profitable projects, but at the time Capcom assured it's fans that both games were still in production and would be safe. Well, we can't always get what we want, and both games were cancelled within a few months of Inafune leaving the company. It was heartbreaking for Mega Man fans who were tired of the lack of support of their favorite series.

As a kid I'd always read online about all these games shown at conventions and shows that would eventually be canceled, such as Sonic X-Treme, and would always wonder what it would be like to play one of those games. I've been to tons of conventions and played tons of games, all of which had seen release. When I played Mega Man Universe, to be honest, I wasn't all that impressed. It was a first day buy for me for sure because I love Mega Man games and they've always been addicting guilty pleasures for me, and maybe that's why I wasn't impressed, and maybe that's why nobody was impressed. It was another Mega Man game, and the level/character customization was just an addition that was too little too late. Maybe that's why Inafune left Capcom, they saw that he was putting out this lackluster game and they wanted to stop it before it went too far, same with Legends. But that's an opinion for another blog.

For me, playing Universe will forever be one of the coolest things because I got to play a game that nobody else will ever get to play again.

If I'm not mistaken, I believe it was only shown off at the San Diego Comic Con, New York Comic Con, and Tokyo Game Show in 2010. After convention season, they quietly cancelled it and it hasn't been seen since. Maybe 15,000 people at most have played it outside of development, and I was one of them. That's an experience I will never forget.

Doesn't stop the game from being what it was: same shit, different toilet.

How My Ex Almost Got Me Killed

It's been a while since I told one of my crazy stories from my troubled youth, so I figured I should finally tell the one story I erroneously forgot to include in Slacker's Paradise that I REALLY regret not including in my book. It's about the time I almost got killed by my ex-girlfriend's psychotic new boyfriend.

I was maybe about 14 or 15 when I started dating this girl Morgan. She was about an inch shorter than me, short black hair, curvy body, HUGE knockers, not a bad body. The day I met her I had forgotten my glasses at home, so I didn't really get a good look at her face due to me being blind as a bat. We were hanging out with all my skateboard bros and just chillin', and she was just really cool. Later that night she asked me if I wanted to be her boyfriend and I said sure, so we were dating officially (or as much as 15 year olds could be).

The next day I HAD my glasses with me, and let me tell you something, when I saw her face through corrective lenses I was shocked. She seemed pretty cute when I first saw her WITHOUT the glasses, but with them? She looked like Two-Face. Actually, she looked like a porcelain vase which has been smashed with an aluminum bat and the pieces all fell into place. Her face was LITERALLY smashed with an aluminum bat and the pieces of her face fell back into place, but the damage had been done. Kinda like Jigsaw from The Punisher. Point is, she wasn't too pleasant to look at, though her face resembled what would've been an attractive face had she not been bludgeoned with the ugly bat. Unfortunately I was smitten, not really, more like I had a heart and actually liked who she was on the inside.

Well, as all teenage relationships do, we broke up after a while. No big deal really. But what would happen next would put her, as well as myself, in great danger. Not long after we ended it, she started dating this 25 year old guy named Cory. Now remember, she's maybe 15 or 16 when this is happening. He was twice my size and twice as angry, this guy was a total nut case. His mom was constantly kicking him out of his house, so he was always sleeping around with various girls just so he can stay over their houses. He was the kind of guy who liked to take advantage of young girls for his own enjoyment.

I more or less stopped talking to her by this point because I wanted nothing to do with this guy, I tried to explain to her that he's no good and he'll never love her the way she wants, but she wouldn't listen. Truth be told I was the only guy she ever dated who WASN'T an asshole to her, but we broke up because we didn't have much in common. It wasn't my problem that she started dating him, but I still felt bad for some reason.

After about a year of mental, emotional, and physical abuse she finally worked up the courage to break up with him, and as usual I was there to pick up the pieces. She was alright about it, but I hung out with her anyways and we took a walk through town so she could get her mind off the situation. As we're walking she keeps getting text messages from him saying he's gonna kill himself and that he'll never love again, same old bullshit every manipulative asshole tries to pull. I tell her to let him kill himself, the world would be a better place with one less asshole. She, unfortunately, didn't feel the same way and felt bad for him.

Apparently it was a very small world as he saw that me and her were walking together as he was driving down the street, so he parks his car and hides somewhere and tells her to get away from me or he's gonna come out and kick my ass. So I did what any coward would do, and I ran into the Blockbuster that we had just past. What? I was fucking 15, he was fucking 25, he was twice my size, what was I supposed to do?!

So I'm watching from the Blockbuster window as she gets in his car and drives away and boy do I feel like an asshole. I just fed my friend to the wolves. She texts me and tells me she's okay and that she would've been worse if I'd stuck around, so I guess it was a smart move. I figure it's safe for me to leave, so I start walking home. Half a mile down the road, who do I see standing in the middle of the parking lot I like to cut through?

They were standing in the middle of the empty parking lot screaming at each other, lucky for her he didn't look too violent though. I thought I could sneak around them and leave, but he spotted me so I ducked into the pharmacy they were shouting in front of. Immediately my phone starts buzzin', she's texting me like crazy saying he's gonna come in and kill me.

Lucky for me, though, there's a very cute girl behind the counter! I would SO be hoppin' on that if it weren't for the fact that MY FUCKING LIFE IS AT STAKE! Though, that didn't stop me from hitting on her. She asked if I needed any help, and I go "Yeah that big dude out there is gonna kill me, you wanna fight my battles for me?" and she laughed and asked me about what happened. I told her the story and finished it off with "if I survive this night, you wanna maybe hang out sometime?" She wrote down her number on a piece of paper and I stuck it in my pocket, at least one thing went right that night.

So I called my buddy Korey (what a co-ink-e-dink) and told him the situation and told him to pick me up at the pharmacy. He speeds up in five minutes and opens the passenger door and says "You fucking asshole, you don't talk to me in a year and now suddenly when you need my help you call me up?" I dive into the car and go "you don't understand what a relief it is to see you." He then asks where they were, and we looked around the lot and they were gone. We were in the clear! We start making our way out of the lot when the unexpected happened.

He was parked on the side of the building hiding, waiting for us to come out, and he started following us. This psychopath was gonna follow us home and probably kick our asses in the comfort of our own living rooms. We didn't want to lead him that way, so we went the opposite direction and tried to lose him. He chased us all over town that night, he was right on our ass the whole time. We eventually shook him when we went through a residential neighborhood, so we pulled into the ShopRite parking lot to cool off and I could fill him in on what happened.

As we're pulling in, it starts snowing heavily and this dude comes sliding in diagonally in front of us and stops the car. He then lunges out of the car and leaps onto the hood of Korey's car and screams at us. "GET THE FUCK OUT OF THE CAR!" He's yelling violently. I look at Korey and he looks at me. "Do it." I say to him.

Korey hits reverse and floors it, sending this psychopathic Hulk flying off the hood. He tumbles onto the ground and starts chasing us on foot. Korey flips the car around and we juice out of there as fast as we can, eventually losing sight of him.

We pulled into the nearby Hess station, finally able to cool off. We run into the Hess Mini-Mart and I'm freaking out, I'm yelling at him about calling the cops, I'm worried about what my mom's gonna say, needless to say I'm freaked. I then got a text message from the girl saying that if I don't come talk to him he's gonna torch my mom's house. Needless to say, THAT freaks me the fuck out.

We went straight to the police station and did a report, told them everything that happened, and they sent their finest officers to the girl's house and when they showed up they arrested the dude and they held him for the weekend in the dirtiest cell they could find. At least I hope it was dirty. After that night I never talked to that girl again, she was on her own.

Every now and then when I log onto Facebook, his face pops up in my "People You May Know". Sometimes I fucking hate Facebook.

PREFACE TO MY CONTROVERSIAL KOTAKU ARTICLE

Back in February of 2012 I wrote an article for the video game news blog Kotaku which has landed me in a LOT of hot water. The idea of the article was I was going to tell a silly story from my sex life, as has been Kail tradition since day one, as a satire on the traditional stereotypical gamer. Nobody got the joke, and everyone fucking exploded on me. How can I blame them, satire is a type of humor only enjoyed by us higher beings. Feels good, doesn't it?

The following is a reprinting of the entire article, as well as my response in defense to the controversy. Honestly, it isn't a typical Kail article, as I had to keep it under 600 words (difficult for the man who likes to talk about himself more than he should), and I didn't want to be too offensive. Believe me, had I done a standard blog for Kotaku the pitchforks would've been sharpened and this book would have been published posthumously. There's still a chance that might happen, but I'm going to hope for the best here.

Anyways, enjoy what was my first, and possibly last, time writing for a major news website! Here it is in full, *How I Achieved Greatness on a Sonic the Hedgehog Themed Bed.*

How I Achieved Greatness on a Sonic Themed Bed

Sonic fans sometimes have a notorious reputation among the general internet populace that we're terribly annoying, way too demanding, and that we have an unwarranted sense of entitlement. As a fan, I can boldly proclaim that while all of that is 100 percent factual (in an opinion kind of way), I can also say that I'm the only Sonic fan, nay, the only gamer to get a girl to sleep with me upon a bed of Sonic.

I moved out of my parent's house at the ripe age of 20, and let me tell you something, it was the best move I've ever made. At home I had rules and regulations on how I was to enjoy myself (bringing girls to my room was a big no-no) so I did the only logical thing and hit the road. At my new place I was a free man, a man who was free to decorate his room the way he felt a man-cave should look: covered from head to toe in Sonic the Hedgehog memorabilia. Action figures still in their packaging lined the walls, a poster of Eddie Lebron's live-action fan film starring Jaleel White in the kitchen, and the cream of the crop – a giant Sonic the Hedgehog throw blanket with matching pillow cases on my bed.

Now, one might take a look at such an apartment and immediately declare "this guy will never get laid," As a self-proclaimed ladies-man, I made it my job to disprove such a theory. I believe that any guy can land any kind of girl if he's both confident and true to himself, so when I found acting like a fool wasn't working, I decided it was time for change. I tried online dating, checked out a few girls, and got checked out myself. One girl in particular was cute, funny, smart, and most-notable-in-the-context-of-this-article, wasn't a nerd at all. Another thing that caught my eye – she had never dated a nerd before.

We met up at the local Starbucks where we got to know each other over some coffee, nothing big. There was definitely a mutual attraction going on, mostly because neither of us made the "date" out to be more than it was. I treated her like I would treat any of my friends, which made her feel really comfortable. She thought it was cool how I just did my own thing, and she was really interested in my comedy. I was confident about myself, and she instantly dug that.

I invited her over my apartment, and of course she wanted to see my bedroom. She broke out into hysterical laughter at my over-the-top Sonic the Hedgehog room, and I will admit I was a little embarrassed at first, but she was totally into it. She thought it was endearing, in a way. We then had sex on the fabled Sonic the Hedgehog blanket, and it was good.

Trust me, she wasn't the only one to enjoy His Royal Kailness upon such luxuries. In fact, there were many others (which you can read about in my book Slacker's Paradise). The truth is, if you're a nerd, geek, gamer, lamer, whatever – you can get the girl. Interests don't matter much in the end, the best way to get a girl interested is to be confident in yourself, don't try so hard, and make sure they feel comfortable. Remember my golden rule – A.B.C, Always Be Closing.

My next goal is to decorate my room in My Little Pony: Friendship is Magic memorabilia and see if my girlfriend doesn't make me sleep in the yard for a week. Once you get tied down everything starts looking more and more like an episode of Everybody Loves Raymond.

The man, the myth, the legend.

In Defense of my Kotaku Article

This is coming a few days late, I realize, but both me and Katie have been incredibly sick the past few days and I've just not been able to get to my computer. During this time, from the luxury of my iPad while dying in bed, I've witnessed numerous accounts of people calling me sexist, misogynistic, chauvinistic, and even possibly a rapist in response to a silly article I wrote for Kotaku about how I had sex with a girl once on a Sonic bed. Time to defend myself.

First off, for those of you who aren't aware, I wrote an article for Kotaku entitled "How I Achieved Greatness on a Sonic the Hedgehog Themed Bed". It was a satirical piece pointing out how stereotypical gamers like to brag about shit that doesn't really matter in the end. AFTER THAT SENTENCE I SHOULD NOT HAVE TO DEFEND MYSELF ANY FURTHER AS THAT SEALS THE DEAL, BUT I SHALL CONTINUE.

While here on the Burger Joint I'll often post funny stories for the sake of posting funny stories, I did that Kotaku article just to make fun of gamers who take pride in stuff that really doesn't matter. Most of the people missed the joke, the article itself wasn't meant to be a laugh riot, it was meant to make you step back and look at gamer culture and realize how silly the gamer stereotype is. "BREAKING NEWS: NERD HAS SEX" That's essentially the gist of it.

What happened after the article went up can only be described as the biggest overreaction since George Lucas receiving death threats over The Phantom Menace. People were going absolutely ape shit on Twitter saying how sexist and misogynistic I was, how it's an outrage that the article even got published, how Kotaku's really lowered their standards, it was INCREDIBLE. People were even dissecting the stories on my website and laying out claims that I'm a rapist because in one story I said how I got the girl to admit that she wanted to have sex with me. Apparently I was "pressuring" her which means I raped her. Last time I checked rape is when you run up to someone, grab them, and force your cock somewhere inside them uncomfortably. What I did was called "making sure she wanted to do it". How the Hell else do you have sex? Am I supposed to wait for the girl to jump on me and have her way with me? Isn't that rape though? Oh wait, just like how there's no such thing as racism towards white people, a man can't be raped by a woman. Silly me.

Other people were saying I was a horrible person for writing a story about a girl that she'll have to read and feel embarrassed for. "Oh, that poor girl, how is she going to show her face in public now?" Newsflash: I DIDN'T USE HER REAL NAME. I DIDN'T USE ANY NAME. I DIDN'T EVEN PUBLISH IT UNDER MY REAL NAME. Kris Kail is a pseudonym. Also, she was well aware that I was a comedian and that I did shit like this before it even happened, and she still had sex with me!

Let's take a serious look at my article. The whole time I talk about the girl I said nothing but nice things about her, and above all else, I mentioned how she wasn't a nerd but found it endearing that I was. There was a mutual attraction going on between too like-minded adults. She came to my place, laughed at my room, and then we had consensual sex. I am not a rapist, but if you're a long time Kail fan obviously I don't need to tell you that.

There are three types of people who read my article: those who thought I was a pig and wanted me dead, those who understood what I was saying and just didn't find it funny, and those who loved it. To those who loved it, I thank you. To those who understood it, and just didn't like it, I thank you too for at least giving it a shot. To those who hated it because they didn't understand it and just want to hate - go fuck yourselves and die in a barrel of bees. You're not my audience.

Am I mad about the controversy? No. Am I mad that I bombed in front of 38,000 people? No, because I didn't bomb in front of 38,000 people, just two-thirds of that 38,000. Probably not even that much. The site got a boatload of traffic the day the article went up, and even after that it's still chuggin' along strong. I jumped from just under 1,000 followers on Twitter to 6,000. I'm obviously doing pretty well for myself. I also sold a bunch of copies of Slacker's Paradise.

If you follow my Twitter (which you should), you'd see exactly how I reacted when it happened. I retweeted every tweet from every angry person, I even got Destructoid's Jim Sterling to call me a sleaze-ball. If you'll recall, Jim Sterling has been a HIGHLY controversial figure in gaming journalism because he's a highly-opinionated asshole. My specific beef with him was that he'd given Sonic Colors, the first truly great Sonic game since 1994, a 4.5 out of 10, and then not 6 months later accepted a one out of 1,000, unavailable to the public, Sonic the Hedgehog 20th Anniversary statue from SEGA.

"Kotaku's story about 'getting laid' is why I see every one of Kotaku's stories about sexism and LGBT stuff as cynically insincere." Jim Sterling, talking about my article.

"Hey, Jim. Glad you liked my article. Would you rate it a 4.5/10 like you did Sonic Colors?" My Response.

"I gotta give @DudeGurlz his due. Me giving a videogame a below average score *is* far sleazier than his Kotaku article." Jim's indirect reply, ripe with sarcasm. "Glad he remembers my article over a year after the fact though, a sentiment I *cannot* say will be true on my end." Again. He knew what I was talking about, so obviously he remembers.

The reason why I'm bringing up what people've said about my article is because there have been NUMEROUS attempts at cashing-in on the controversy. Some low-level bloggers have been writing articles bashing me for being exactly what I wrote the article against, as well as people claiming I'm outright unfunny. That last part, alright, I can't fight that. Everyone's got an opinion on what's funny and what's not funny, but the fact that people are literally trying to cash-in on the controversy, that's what's pissing me off. I refuse to reveal who they are as I don't want their tactics to work in their favor, but I will say that there were a few who stand out in my mind.

By the way, my article only reached 38,000 views BECAUSE of the outrage. Most Kotaku articles reach around 1,000 to 5,000 views, but mine quadrupled that. Why? Because everyone on Twitter crying and saying "I DON'T WANT TO GIVE KOTAKU THE VIEWS BUT THIS KID TALKED ABOUT HAVING SEX ON A SONIC BED." If nobody had complained about it, the whole thing would've been a bust and I wouldn't have sold as many books as I've sold.

Honestly, I didn't think this whole thing would've been a big deal. I expected a few thumbs up, sell maybe ten copies of the book, and then people forget about it, but this thing has blown up to a level beyond what I expected. Feels good man.

CHAPTER 5
THE KING OF SPRING BREAK

CLINTON ROAD

I graduated high school in June of 2008 and immediately after began my summer-time merriment. At the time I was hanging out with The Collective We, which was my cool kid gang composed of Alex Goldstein, Tom Malach, Cesar and Danny Arakaki (all from the band Harpoon Forever), Nick Weinbrecht (aka Dubs), Chris Romags, Chris Catoya, Ramy Youssef (now an aspiring comedian with a decent following) Derek Spaldo (now an actor acting in various commercials, music videos, plays, and bit parts), Vin Landolfi (who plays guitar for Lauriana Mae), and Andrew Teller (my co-host from Destroy All Slackers). That whole summer we were all the best friends, we hung out every day, occasionally swapping who was where or with who.

Every day we would just meet up at a mutual spot and either went out to a diner, Applebee's, or White Castle, or we'd just drive around town, or we'd hang out at someone's house. The main thing that kept us together as a group of friends was our collective sense of humor and our joint love of music. You see, at the time Alex, Ramy, Tom, Derek, and Sos were in a band called Alex and the Horribles, and I was doing the Kail music solo. This mutual friendship between bands made it easy to go out and hang as a group, especially since if they were playing a show I'd usually open for them. This went on until they became a medium-time band playing shows in Brooklyn at venues like Death By Audio, as venues like that are way too cool for a nerd rocker like Kail.

But back in Rutherford when the guitars were away, we were always doing crazy shit. One night right after graduation Chris Catoya pulled up with his mom's mini-van and said "Pile in, guys! We're going to Clinton Road!" Which is how he'd remember it, truth be told I egged him on to get his mom's mini-van and take us to Clinton Road, as he was the only one with access to a car and a driver's license. I think it was me, Tom, Derek, Alex, and Romags who got into the car that night, but I might be mistaken. Doesn't matter who was there, really, point was we were gonna go chase ghosts!

A little background on Clinton Road first. Here in New Jersey we have a magazine called Weird NJ that exposes the scariest, creepiest, weirdest, most haunted corners of New Jersey. It's an immensely popular magazine that's gone on to produce books for individual states and even the entire country. If you live in Jersey, chances are you've gone on a "Weird NJ" trip at one point or another. Clinton Road was featured in the magazine and is one of the most popular destinations because of its easy access from the highway. It's right off of Route 23 in West Milford, and it's only scary because it's literally 5 miles of winding, dangerous road that connects West Milford to Upper Greenwood Lake. Did I mention there's not a single road light the entire way through? Driving down Clinton Road late at night tends to be one of the scariest things you could do next to taking a late night drive through Newark or Camden. There are myths that it's a haunted road plagued with ghosts, Satanists, Klansmen, Nazis, witches, cannibals, and rednecks. Only the last one is true, as with any neighborhood written about in Weird NJ, if you drive through this way and stop anywhere you will get shot at by rednecks who hate tourists.

Knowing this, we decided to take the 40 minute car ride up to Clinton Road. The whole car ride up we talked about wrestling, listened to Barry White (from Catoya's mom's collection of CDs), and laughed our asses off at nothing. It wasn't until we got to Clinton Road that we decided to scare ourselves by turning the music all the way down so we couldn't hear anything but our own breathing. Catoya slowed the car down and we looked out the windows at all the "ghosts" and "demons" that weren't there, but hilariously enough there was a lot of Satanic graffiti to make one believe the place was haunted. As we went, I felt nature's call and told Catman I needed to take a leak, so we pulled off to the side and I got out and went to the woods and pulled out the snake. As I was about to unload, the guys thought it would be hilarious to pull off without me. There's nothing scarier than the idea of being abandoned in the middle of the woods in the middle of the night, especially a supposedly haunted wooded area.

I chased them down and was screaming words that would make my poor mother cry until they stopped. I gleefully caught up to the car, and they started driving again. That old trick! They stopped for real and let me in, oh man was I pissed. They were all laughing hysterically at me while I completely forgot I had to piss. What a miserable night. Not long after we decided we were gonna pack it in, so the Catman made a U-turn and we headed off for home. Maybe a few minutes go by and this car pulls up behind us and starts tailgating us. Thinking it's some kids up there doing the same thing as us, we ignored them and just kept heading home. Not a few minutes go by and they start getting right up our ass, so Catman pulls to the side to let them pass, but they pull to the side with us. We get scared for a second thinking they're rednecks about to kick our asses, when the red and blue lights go on and we realize it's a cop. Another thing about Clinton Road, it's notorious for cops who're low on tickets for the month. If you're a West Milford cop and you need to get your quota up, the best place to go is Clinton Road because you're more than likely to find some kids breaking the law. What our cop found was a provisional driver with more than one person in the car. He got a ticket that he foolishly tried to fight, and we were sent home.

When we got back to Rutherford the Catman decided he was gonna head home, but we still wanted to hang out. It was only 2 A.M. and the night was still young! So he dropped us off by a park on a hill and

Ramy, Catoya, and the sexiest gentleman in the world.

went on his merry way to face his parents who were gonna rip him a new one for getting a ticket. We decided we were gonna keep ghost hunting, even if we had to make up our own stories, but first thing was first: I still had to piss, and BADLY. We were in a park, it was 2 A.M., I said fuck it and decided to just piss right there. "Hey, guys! Don't nobody come over here, I'm taking a piss!" I yelled at the guys to make sure they didn't look at my hog as I pulled it out. Finally able to enjoy my piss, I let out a nice sigh of relief, and not a minute too soon. As I'm letting out that sigh, though, I hear a girl's voice go "ewwwww!" I look over at a park bench not two feet away and there's two girls sitting there. I go "C'mon! I gave fair warning before I pulled it out!" to them, finish up, and I booked it as fast as I could away from there.

I told the guys what had happened and they all laughed hysterically at me. Not a single thing could go right that night, so I figured it was time to pack the fuck up and head home. I applied the skin to my respective bros, and moseyed my way home. On the way I stopped at 7-11 and got myself a large Slurpee and some Slim-Jims. I figured I wasn't going to be falling asleep any time soon, so why not stock up on snacks for when I surf 4chan and jerk off to porn? It wound up being an awesome night.

THE MOST ANNOYING BITCH IN THE WORLD

One thing I always loved about the Collective was that me and Alex were pretty much the glue that brought everyone together. The reason for that was because in high school we all hung out with different crowds, and we just knew each other in passing. The only reason why I knew Sos was because his gym locker was next to mine my Freshman/his Sophomore year. He played drums and found himself in Alex's band with Derek and Ramy, who I knew from doing the plays in high school. Alex I've known since the fourth grade and had always been tight with, but he's the real reason I hung out with those guys at this time. Nick Dubs was also real tight with Alex, which is why he hung out with the crew even though he was primarily a jock in high school. I guess mostly Alex was the glue, but doesn't matter, I was still in the crew.

One thing I always loved about our group was how accepting we were of new dudes to hang out with us. Every now and then one of us would invite an outside friend to hang out, and eventually they'd become one of us. The weirdest part was when, for example, I would invite one of my outside friends and then someone I wasn't as close to in the group would become best friends with that dude. I always liked that, but I always found it strange in a way. Unfortunately for me, though, on one such occasion Sos invited one of his friends to hang out with us who I couldn't stand.

Her name was Christina, and she was a bitch. Plain and simple. She was short, maybe barely five foot even, she looked like she was Asian, but I'm not sure that she was, and she was a total hipster. She lived in San Francisco and lived the glamorous life of a total cool kid. In high school she had made herself known as the loud one who wanted everyone's attention, she'd be super sweet to the people she wanted to be friends with and anyone who she disliked got treated like absolute shit. She once told a friend of mine to get raped just because she didn't like the cut of her jib (that's a line I stole from Animal Crossing). Her problem with me? I was more likable than she was.

In the Collective I was the loud jokester who was always going on and on about how 2001 was the best year for music. I constantly wore this oversized Limp Bizkit t-shirt Alex bought me, I listened to nothing but Staind, Korn, Linkin Park, P.O.D., Saliva, Drowning Pool, and Puddle of Mudd, and I would not shut up about movies like American Pie and Dude Where's My Car. I always had to be the center of attention, that was my role in the group. Everybody always had Kail-isms and Kail related jokes to tell, and I loved every minute of it.

At one point during the Summer of 2008 Christina had come back to Rutherford to visit for a few weeks, and she was best friends with Sos back in the day, and he even knew she was a total bitch. He admitted to me that he only hung out with her out of loyalty. He started bringing her along to hang out with us and when she came she wouldn't just pipe down and hang out to the side like a good hanger-on. No, instead she had to raise her stupid whiney voice and cry for attention. I was working at Blockbuster at the time, so I didn't get to really hang out every night. I didn't know she was in town, so when I had a day off I called Sos, met up with the crew, and to my surprise there she was. I was civil with her at first, but eventually she brought me to my boiling point, which is something you gotta really work for.

One of our biggest problems as a group was deciding what it was we were gonna do for the night. Were we going bowling? Were we getting half-off-apps at Applebee's? Was it gonna be a midnight in Kail's basement playing Dreamcast? Every night we spent at least two hours hanging out on the street or at a park figuring this out, we could never just settle on White Castle like I always suggested. This one night in particular, Christina was being especially loud and annoying as we were walking through town. She was bored with us not being able to settle on something to do, so she suggested we go to Applebee's. I wholeheartedly agreed with her and supported this idea, but our calls fell on deaf ears. No one was interested in going anywhere that night.

Eventually she gave up on trying to get them to do anything, but I was starving. We'd been walking around town all night and I wanted to get some good eats in my belly. "Are we fucking going to a diner or Applebee's or something? I'm just tryin'a get me some good eats!" I said to the group. "Shut the fuck up already, Kris! God, you're so fucking annoying!" Christina politely screamed at me. Politely isn't the word I wanted to use, but I couldn't figure out a way to make an adjective out of cunt.

I looked at her and I went "Christina nobody ever wanted you here in the fucking first place, we were glad to be rid of you after high school when you moved to San Francisco and we're more than excited to have you go the fuck home!"

Alex had to hold me back for what would happen next because after I exclaimed that rather loudly, she started going off on me. She was saying how she was their friend first, I came out of nowhere, I was a nothing, a nobody, etc. From the looks of it, it looked like she was going to start taking swings at me. A general rule of thumb for me has been to never hit a woman, but she was FAR from a woman. She was a little rotten cunt who deserved to be given oral pleasure by a homeless guy with bleeding gums and a case of the AIDS. I told myself not to do anything silly, and to only hit her if she strikes first. I was hoping she'd do it, but she didn't. Sos calmed her down and she demanded he drive her home, so he did and then I yelled at Alex for holding me back. Really he was protecting me from myself, as I would've made a right ass out of myself. Unfortunately, even though everyone in town hated her and her own parents shipped her off to San Francisco to get rid of her, punching her would've made me look like a major jerk off for some reason. I really don't understand the world sometimes.

After that night the group went out to Applebee's without me, they had invited me, but I couldn't go because of work. Christina went with them, and in my place was Sos's Uncle Danny, who we affectionately refer to as Drunkle D because he's always drinking wine and singing hair metal wildly. I find this amusing because the main doesn't have a single hair on his head, he kind of reminds me of a mixture of Lou from Hot Tub Time Machine and Uncle Fester. He's a real trip, and fortunately for me Christina liked him just about as much as she liked me.

From what everyone tells me, that night was the best night ever because Drunkle D was able to finish the job I'd started: getting her ass back to San Francisco and never coming to New Jersey again. Every time she opened her mouth Drunkle D had a comment to make about how stupid and annoying she was, and if you guys think I'm obnoxious you should spend five minutes with this guy. He makes me look like a saint. At one point in the night he was finally fed up with her nonsense and told her to shut the fuck up and then he proceeded to call her a cunt, which in the world of insulting women equates to Daigo kicking Justin Wong's ass in Street Fighter III: 3rd Strike with only one pixel of health remaining.

After that night I never heard from her again, so I guess Drunkle D must have really slayed the dragon. According to rumors, he was so proud of himself (or drunk out of his mind) that he tipped the waiter $80 and paid for everyone's meals. He will always be my hero for avenging me after I was made to look like a fool in front of my peers (note: when writing peers I accidentally wrote beers and laughed for a good couple of minutes).

The First Annual Kailbecue

Every summer my family would go down the shore, and seeing as I always hated the beach I felt it'd be appropriate to skip out on this family vacation every time it came up. Usually my excuse was that I was working, but truth be told I never really had a job. So I'd get the house to myself for a week, which meant I had to do something big each time. The first year I had the house all to myself I threw what would become the annual Kailbecue – a whole night of gurlz, lunch, and money open to all who could make it. It was going to be legendary.

The summer of 2008 was when I first started working at Blockbuster, and since I was new they started me out working once or twice a week, so that week that my family went down the shore would be mine. My friend Danii (who was a girl) wanted to hang out, and she had this friend with her named Shawnee (also a girl) who wanted to meet me. I don't know if she actually wanted to meet me, but I was interested in gurlz. They came over around 5 in the afternoon and we hung out in my basement watching TV, just the three of us shootin' the bull. Shawnee was pretty hot, apparently she was South African, but for some reason she was white. I didn't know there was white people in South Africa at the time, you see it'd be another year before District 9 came out, but damn was she hot. This was the day Alex had gotten me my legendary Limp Bizkit t-shirt from the local Salvation Army, so I was wearing it with pride hopin' Shawnee would be impressed by my awesome fashion sense.

At one point Danii suggested we go to Chris's Pizza and visit Sos (he was a delivery boy there at the time, and still is now thinkin' about it), so we went out to grab a slice and hang out with the big S. Sos totally agreed with me that Shawnee was hot, and he told me to totally achieve with her. That was the plan, of course, as I always say – ABC, always be closing! Sos told us he was about to get out of work, and asked if we wanted to hang out afterword. I told him to stop by Shop Rite and pick up some burgers and dogs and we could have a barbecue in the backyard. I called up some more friends and they met us at the house and we all hung out in the basement playing guitar and telling jokes while Godzilla movies played in the background on the TV.

After Sos got out of work he swung by the house with food in tow and started grillin' up some mean steamed hams (that's what they call hamburgers in Albany). By this point Danii'd called up some of her female friends, so there was a good amount of gurlz there, but the whole time I had my eye on Shawnee. At one point one of my bros called asking for a favor, he'd been hanging out with this chick he met at a film school program and the last train home for her had already come and gone, so she was stuck in Rutherford. He couldn't let her crash at his place because his parents were around, and he couldn't drive her home because he didn't have a car, so essentially he was up shit's creek without a paddle. He called Tom, but Tom couldn't help him out, luckily Kail had a whole empty house that nobody was sleeping in that night.

I took the phone from Tom and told the unnamed bro that he could bring her down by me and she could spend the night here, of course this is after Tom had told me she was apparently one of the hottest girls he'd ever seen. Would I really break Bro Code with one of my closest bros? I'd already broken the Bro Code with him before, why not do it again? So I told him she'd be totally safe here from any would be attackers, but of course I made no promises about not hitting on her myself.

Sos was gonna go pick them up, and for some reason Danii wanted to go with him, and so did the rest of the party. I don't remember how, but for a good half hour me and Shawnee were in my basement alone together. She was playing guitar and I was sitting at my computer talking to a friend of mine over AIM asking him what I should do. He told me to stop fucking talking to him and start fucking talking to her, and his advice I did take. Shawnee was playing the Bob Dylan song Knocking on Heaven's Door, which I knew by heart, so I started singing along with her, but I made a few adjustments to the lyrics.

"Mama take this badge offa me, I can't use it any more, it's getting hard, too hard to see, feel I'm knockin' up a stupid whore. Knock, knock, knockin' up a stupid whore... knock, knock, knockin' up a stupid whore."

When I started singing I had her, but when I changed the lyrics to fit my rather unusual personality I'd lost her. She put down the guitar and stomped out of the room, obviously I wasn't about to dip my wick in her boobs tonight or any night.

Luckily for me, the gang had return with my unnamed bro and his very lusty date. When Tom said she was incredibly hot he wasn't lyin'. She had a blonde/brown emo haircut, dark eyeliner, snake-bite piercings, a white tank top, dark blue skinny jeans, and the curviest body I've ever seen, it was like a perfect hour-glass figure. They joined our party and we got to know her, she was pretty cool, and she was comfortable staying the night until she really got to know our group. For some reason Sos wanted to take a shower, maybe he was sweaty, maybe he just needed to get the pizza and burger scent off him, I don't know, but he took a shower and came downstairs in only his underwear, so I decided to join him and I dropped trou. We then chased everyone around the basement trying to hug whoever'd let us, it was great. Everyone thought it was hilarious.

As these shenanigans were going on, Danii went to the new girl and told her that if she wanted to she could spend the night at her house to avoid our hi-jinx. What a total cock block, I could've had her, no question about it. But really, it was for the better as Danii helped me avoid breaking

Bro Code with this particular bro for the second time (yes, it's the same bro with whom I'd broken code with earlier in the book).

At the end of the night the only one who wanted to spend the night was Derek, who lived a block up the road anyways. He even went home to get pajamas and his toothbrush. Not that I minded, he's a great friend, but damn I was hoping to get laid that night. Oh well, better luck next year.

THE SECOND ANNUAL KAILBECUE

A year later, I was still working a dead end job that for some reason I loved. I worked at my local Blockbuster. What could be better than that? Free movie rentals, tons of video games to play, all the girls coming in and out of the store. Nothing could ever top working at that video store. There was one specific Sunday night I will never forget when I worked at that video store.

It was a slow night, me and my pal Jay-Rey (you may remember him from the podcast Kill the Queen) were busy working, by working I mean I was buying candy and popcorn under my second account so I could rack up some numbers for the week without actually harassing the customers, and he was figuring out a movie we could put on instead of watching the stupid trailer-reel. We were having a conversation about video games when she walked in. This beautiful girl, pale white skin covered in tattoos, short black hair, bright blue eyes, gorgeous smile, cutest little black dress, she was a full-blown ten.

At the time I was horribly awkward, but as luck would have it she came up to me. She asked me if I could help her find a specific movie, so I checked the computer and it said we didn't have it, but just to get a chance to talk to her I told her there might be one copy and I'd help her find it.

We went into the Drama section, which was luckily empty, and I asked her what kind of movies she liked. Right about now you're probably thinking how suave I must've been, well, you'd be wrong as I was nervous, sweaty, and stumbling over my words. But she went along with it, obviously aware that I was hitting on her. It might've been the nervousness, or the socially awkward aspect of my character, or maybe the red hair, but for some reason she thought I was cute.

As I knew would happen, we didn't find the movie she wanted, but I offered to suggest a similar movie for her. She turned down my suggestion, but asked if we had another movie, which we did. I rung her up and told her my name and said we should hang out at some point, and by this time I'm not as nervous as I was before. She giggled and said sure, and she gave me her phone number. I couldn't tell you how excited I was, I immediately ran over to Jay-Rey to tell him.

Unfortunately, he didn't catch a glimpse of her because he was busy being Mr. Manager. I had to explain how cute she was, and the whole time he was rolling his eyes going "Oh, that Kail, and his silly stories of hot girls giving him their phone numbers." But she was real! He laughed and jokingly said "She probably isn't as hot as you make her out to be, she's probably just another Kail gurl." What Jay-Rey doesn't understand is that Kail gurlz are ALWAYS hot! Wow, that's a bold faced lie, I'm sorry.

Anyways, the next day I texted her and we started talking more about movies. She was into the classics, old black and white movies from the 30's and 40's. We went on and on through text for hours just getting to know each other, and I could tell she was really cool. I started getting a little crush on her, admittedly, and I needed an excuse to hang out with her.

The time of year had come where my family went down the shore for a week on vacation, which gave me the perfect opportunity to throw another Kailbecue as an excuse to hang out with this chick. I called up Sos, told him the situation, and we were on our way to the store to start buying groceries for the party. We grabbed all the things we needed, burgers, dogs, mac 'n cheese, BBQ sauce, jello, a vegetarian platter, the essentials. We were a couple of kings living the good life, buying all the good eats we could get our grubby little hands on.

The day before the party I was having a conversation with the girl through text. I told her about how awesome the barbecue was going to be and I asked her if she wanted to come. If she had said no, all the hard work we put into it would've been for naught. Luckily, though, she excitedly told me she'd love to attend my exciting box social. I had the lead, I just needed to close the deal, and you know my golden rule: ABC – Always Be Closing.

Day of the party and we're setting up for everything, making sure everything's just right. Had it been a normal Kailbecue, I would've just said "fuck it lets wait till the last minute." But this was different, there were GURLZ on the line! With everything set up exactly the way it should be, I left Sos in control of the party while I went to go pick up the girl of my dreams. I found my way to her house and she was wearing the most adorable dress I'd ever seen, and my heart was racing faster than anything. We got to the house and I introduced her around, but apparently all my friends already knew her to my surprise.

We hung around and talked for a while and everything was cool. She seemed to be having a great time, but I found it a bit off-putting when she made a remark about there being no alcohol at the party. Surprised me a little considering I had thought she wasn't big on drinking, but apparently she liked to drink a lot when she went to parties.

At one point she winds up leaving early to go meet up with her friends, which I was cool with. I felt like I royally blew it though, I really should've at least bought beer. I mean, c'mon, what 18 year old has a party at his parents' house and DOESN'T make sure there's plenty of alcohol? I was such a fucking zilch, I could've closed the deal easily and made her my girlfriend if I got her liquored up.

The pieces started falling together when she left, though. My friends all started questioning why I had invited her, asking if I was just looking to get laid. I was puzzled, as they knew at the time I really wasn't like that. I had this cute innocent thing about me at the time where I actually wanted a girlfriend, not just a one night stand. I'm still like that today, even though one night stands regrettably happen, I try to at least push to be in a relationship. Apparently they thought that wasn't the case, as the girl I had brought to meet them all had already been with each and every one of my friends.

Alright, that might be an exaggeration, but everyone did have a story to tell about her. The girl I had thought was a cute, smart, funny, innocent girl wound up being the town whore. In fact, she thought that was why I invited her. Just to get in her pants. I was so embarrassed for weeks after that, not because I invited a whore to my party thinking she was a nice girl to date, but because I didn't even get any out of her! How embarrassing is it to actually attempt to get with the easiest girl on the planet and not actually succeed? I was so humiliated.

Spring Break in Kail's Basement

As I mentioned earlier, the one thing I've been famous for among my group of friends is my obsession with the year 2001. You see, for a brief period of time during the very late 90's and the very early 2000's, maybe from 1999 to 2002, there was an influx of great alternative rock music in the mainstream. Bands like Korn, Limp Bizkit, Staind, Saliva, P.O.D., Linkin Park, The Offspring, Papa Roach, Disturbed, Drowning Pool, Finger Eleven, Rob Zombie, etc. were making it big on MTV and on the radio. At the same time skateboarding, snowboarding, wrestling, and the rest of the extreme sports were really popular, just the whole "extreme" life style was the thing. Doritos and Mountain Dew were where it's at, and if you weren't watching Gundam Wing and Dragon Ball Z on Toonami you weren't cool. It was a good time to be a bro, and 2001 was the high point of this short-lived era.

As time went on, everyone moved on from the whole "extreme" thing, but for one reason or another I didn't. For years after I was still listening to all those bands, watching Dragon Ball Z, and drinking Mountain Dew. This sort of became a joke for my friends, and it got to the point where I made that my persona. I was an anachronism, a dude from 2001 living in 2008.

After the summer ended and my friends had all gone to college, I stayed behind and worked my butt off at Blockbuster. I'll get more into that later, but aside from a few weekends where they came home and we'd hang out, I essentially waited until Winter Break for them to come home. Even though it was Winter Break, for some reason I ran around calling it Spring Break because I wanted to be "EXTREME!" And there was nothing more extreme than Spring Break.

Every night the guys would come over my house after midnight and we'd hang out in my basement playing Puzzle Fighter on my Dreamcast until about 5 in the morning. It started out just me, Cesar, and Sos. We'd go out with the guys to White Castle or something, and then we'd come back to my house after everyone went home and we'd sit there and have these in depth Puzzle Fighter competitions. It was a two player game, so whoever lost during that match would give up the controller to whoever wasn't playing. For a while I was the top dog, but Sos would eventually overthrow me as top dog.

For those of you who don't know, Puzzle Fighter is a puzzle game along the lines of Tetris or Puyo Puyo that was designed by Capcom in the mid-90's as a cutesy puzzle spin-off of their wildly popular Street Fighter series. The idea to the game was to stack colored gems, and you had to connect the same color gems with each other, and when you got an orb in that color and you attached it to your stack of like-color gems, they would break, you'd get points, and your opponent would get stacked with some "timer gems" that would wait three or four turns to become use-able gems. Once you get the hang of it it's really an addicting puzzle game, and it works really well as a multiplayer party game.

The other game we'd play in the basement was Bomberman, and if I have to explain Bomberman to you then you're reading the wrong book, but I'll give it a go. Bomberman is essentially a video game adaptation of the Oklahoma City Bombings from 1995 and you play as a cute Japanese style Timothy McVeigh. You walk around in a maze full of breakable bricks and unbreakable bricks, and you lay out bombs that break bricks and you collect power ups and you try to blow up your friends. Puzzle Fighter was good when you had two friends together, but Bomberman was where it's at if you had a whole crew over.

Eventually everyone would wind up in my basement playing Puzzle Fighter or Bomberman, some dudes would be playing pool on the other side of the basement, and some dudes would be playing guitar. It was a regular party every night, and we would just constantly do this. Going out? Nah forget about it, it was all about video game parties in Kail's basement!

One night in particular that I'll never forget, we were going out to chill with Vinnie and his girlfriend and her friend Victoria. It was me, Sos, and Cesar, and we met up with them at Lincoln Park on Park Ave in Rutherford and we just kind of chilled in Cesar's van and joked around the whole night. At the time I was single, and I was kind of interested in Victoria, so I was putting on the "2001 extreme" act to get her moist. She thought I was hysterical, she absolutely adored my whole "SPRING BREEEEEAKKKKKKKKK" shtick.

The whole time I was half-hitting on her, trying to be nonchalant and cool, but it was just blatantly obvious I wanted her. Let's take a step out of the story for a moment to take a look at something first. When I say I "wanted" someone, at this point in my life I wanted to take them out on a date. Usually when you think of a dude hitting on a girl you think he only wants to hit it and quit it, but it was different with me for some reason. My thing was I always wanted to get a date and see where things went, I was barely interested in sex. Back to the story, she wasn't all that interested in me, but I thought I had a shot.

Around 2 A.M. everyone decides to go home and go to bed, but I was still wide awake, so Sos and Cesar came over my house for some Bomberman. The whole night I was harassing Cesar about Victoria because he was friends with her.

"Dude, do you think she'd be into me?" I'd say to him.

"Dude, I don't know, just go for it, man. Talk to her." He'd reply.

"But, dude! This chick is tops! I need to know if she'd allow me into her proverbial forest!"

Cesar, me, and Sos hanging out in my parent's basement.

"Well, I can't help you there."

So we're playing Bomberman and I hadn't mentioned her in a while, but finally I open my yap again and ask Cesar more questions about her.

"What do you think the brown-to-pink ratio of her bunghole is?"

"What? I don't fucking know man."

"But like, all I want to know is what color her brown eye is. Do you think it's like dark brown because she never wipes and it's just forever stained? Or maybe it's pink and fresh? Is her bung piece bald and fresh, a few hairs sprinkled around the hole, or is it like a gorilla's hairy asshole?"

"Dude! Just fucking find out for yourself! She's probably not all that difficult to get into bed with. Just be cool, and don't be an asshole creep."

"Yeah, but what about her net worth? How much do you think she's valued at?"

"What does that have to do with anything?"

"I need to know if I'm making an investment here."

"Well, thinking about it she does live in a pretty big house, I guess she's worth a bit."

"Alright, so if I get with her and her bung is hairy then it won't be all bad. At least I can milk her for all she's worth."

I then gave up my turn in Puzzle Fighter to go onto my laptop and go on Facebook. I went on her Facebook page and posted a comment on her wall.

"Hey! It was fun hanging out tonight! We should get together again soon!"

The next day she commented saying "Yeah, I had a lot of fun, maybe we'll hang out next SPRING BREEEEEEAKKKK!"

After that I never spoke to her again, maybe she'll pick this book up at Barnes and Noble and decide to contact me and let me know she has a hairless bung piece. I really wish I'd put some effort into that so I could've found out.

A few nights after that the gang was over and we were watching Godzilla movies in the basement. I told them the whole story about what happened with Victoria, and they all thought it was funny. Nick Dubs then proceeded to try to give me advice on how to land a date with a girl and I looked at him and said "Dubs when was the last time you been on a date with anyone?"

He then shot me a look that could only express the Dubs version of human rage.

"SHUT THE FUCK UP, KAIL! YOU DON'T KNOW NOTHIN'!"

I was taken back for a second because Dubs never yelled anything before in his life. Everyone started cracking up and that became the new catchphrase. Whenever someone would say something we'd look at them and go "SHUT THE FUCK UP, YOU DON'T KNOW NOTHIN'!" Dubs was at first a little embarrassed about it, but then came to terms with it and now it's one of his key catchphrases.

Near the end of the night we were still laughing hysterically over Dubs' catchphrase, and I got up to do my Dr. Robotnik impression. I was going to do Dubs as Robotnik, so I got up and started going "Huhuhuahuahua GET A LOAD OF THIS!" and I called up the voice from my stomach a little too hard because something extra came with it and I vomited all over the carpet. All the bros in the room cheered me on as I violently threw up all the White Castle and Doritos and Mountain Dew I had that night. It took me a good half hour to clean it up, but damn if I didn't get the best laughs of my life that night.

Those nights were some of the best nights of our friendship, and I don't think anything could ever compare to them. That's a blatant lie, because before Spring Break, or actually Winter Break as it were, there was a period of time in the Fall of 2008 where we actually left the confines of our houses, and even our humble town of Rutherford, New Jersey, for the parties and shows of Brooklyn.

Death By Audio

The best part about being friends with dudes in bands was that I got to go to all the shows for free as the roadie, and I got to go to all the parties. Alex hates when I tell this story because he doesn't want people to get the idea that he's in a party band, but at the time Alex and the Horribles was an upbeat, fun band to see perform live. Alex was always bouncing around, grabbing random people, and just being silly. At one show he took my glasses off my face and put them on and performed the rest of the show with my glasses on. He definitely had a migraine to end all migraines after that.

Back in September of '08, right after everyone went back to school for the Fall, Alex and the Horribles booked a show at Death by Audio in Williamsburg, Brooklyn. If you didn't already know about this venue before then you'd never know about it because it's so lo-fi it's almost a secret. In reality, the place is a little warehouse that's been fitted to work as a venue. During the day it looks like your typical storage warehouse, but at night when you see a crowd of kids out front you know it's the ultimate hang out spot. You go in and there's a small stage area, the P.A.'s and everything are all set up, and there's the standing area. To the back of the room there's a doorway that leads to a hang out room where there's a guy selling drinks out of a cooler, but just like an old speakeasy, you don't actually buy drinks from him. You buy beads from him, and then you give him the beads and he gives you a beer. Underage? No chance. They were strict about that. There's also a few couches and a bathroom in the hang out area.

I met up with the dudes at the venue an hour before the show started so I could help them unload their stuff and set up. Working as a roadie was about as glamorous as being a writer on SNL – you got to craft something beautiful and amazing, but you got none of the credit. It's okay though, because you get free admission to the shows and you get to hang with the talent, which automatically ups your cool factor. We set up the instruments and equipment on the stage and we had some spare time before the show started, so we were just chillin'. At the time the band was Alex, Tom, Derek, Ramy, and Sos, and I think I was the only one from our crew who came to the show. A few of Tom's friends from college came and they were really cool. After a while we were socializing with everyone there.

It was almost 7:30 and Alex and the Horribles were the first ones up, so they got up to the stage and Alex pulled me aside and said "Dude, this is gonna be one of my best performances. Just you watch. I'm gonna grab that girl over there and make out with her during one of the solos."

"Dude I think she came with a guy though."

"Yeah, but she's not WITH him. I talked to her before, she's cool, and I can tell she's totally into me."

"Alright, man! Go for it, but if you don't do it you know I'll rag on you for the rest of time."

Sure enough, during the set he was flailing around the stage as usual, even jumped off the stage and got inches away from the audience. He was throwing punches, grabbed my glasses again and put them on, and as he said he would, he pulled that girl to him and started making out with her in front of everyone. Alright, it wasn't a huge make out, it was just a kiss, but still. He had balls, and that's something I'll always say about

Alex. His balls didn't come from his wanting to impress people though, it was from his wanting to entertain me. That was his thesis throughout high school, and even into our adult lives he still goes out of his way to try and make me laugh.

After the band's set was over we went back to the hang out area and hung out with the crowd back there. At the time I was still working on the "new Kail album", which was another joke amongst us. I haven't done a full Kail album since April 2008's Humor Songs, and ever since I've been talking about doing a new album. I was so excited over it I was telling everyone about how successful I was, how I had 10,000 MySpace friends, and other bullshit. There were a few dudes there that were impressed with me and wanted to keep in contact, so I gave them my MySpace and they never added me.

Eventually Tom's friend invited us all to his apartment for the after party, and we went over and it was awesome. He'd called up all the girls he knew, they came down, brought pot, and we all hung out. Alex spent the night hangin' with the girl he kissed at the show, I was proud of him, he'd achieved before I did that night. Me and Sos smoked up with a few dudes, this being the first time I really tried pot. It was a good time with good friends, and the whole time I was laughing my ass off. At one point, me and Sos were sitting behind the couch just kind of chillin' and these two girls come up and sit by us, one by me and the other by Sos.

I don't remember the other chick, but the one who sat by me was really cute. She had an innocent looking girl next door face, short black hair, blue eyes, red lipstick, and she was a little thick and curvy. When I say thick I don't mean she was fat, she was maybe just a little bit under chubby. Her name was Dani (not to be confused with Danii, who's the chick I went to high school with who took my notes for me after the midnight premiere of Star Wars), and I was totally sold on her.

I struck up a conversation with her and she was really cool, but I was too nervous to really get into anything with her. Eventually Sos started freaking out because he was so stoned, so he went into the kitchen and laid down on the floor. He was so out of it he later told me he imagined a dude walking into the kitchen and that moment lasted for like

Alex, Derek, Danny, and Tom in Harpoon Forever. Unfortunately I didn't have a picture of Alex and the Horribles, so this'll have to do.

an hour. As I was trying to get to know this totally rockin' babe so that I might take her out on a nice dinner date at some point, Derek came over and totally cock blocked me.

"Dude, I think there's something wrong with Sos, we should go grab him and head back to New Jersey."

"Dude, D-Double-Dawg-Derek, he's totally fine."

"Dude, Kail, seriously I think Sos needs to get home."

Whether he was right or not, it doesn't matter, because Sos was my bro and I couldn't leave him for grade A tail. I said that at the time and I hate myself for it now because she could've been the love of my life. Me being the idiot that I am, I didn't think to get her number or Facebook her or anything, so I split with the gang. We loaded Sos back into his mom's mini-van, and Ramy drove them home. Because of the instruments being there, there wasn't enough room for me to climb into the van, so I wound up taking the bus home. That's the easy way of explaining it, the more detailed one was a little different.

Being high as a kite, I stumbled my way onto the R train and took it to Times Square where I walked my ass over to McDonalds. At the time I was barely making any money at Blockbuster, so I only had so much money on me. Not caring about this, I totally over drafted my bank account because I had to have two Double-Cheeseburgers with Big Mac sauce, 20 Chicken McNuggets, a large order of fries with extra sweet and sour sauce, and a McCinnabon whatever that thing was, it was like a cinnamon melt thing. Let me tell you guys, it was the best meal I'd ever had. I loved it so much I missed the 1:15 AM bus. Unfortunately for me, the NJ Transit busses run sporadically after midnight. The schedule said the next bus would be coming at 2:15, so no problem, I'd hang out and wait for the clock to strike 2:15 and the 190 would pull up and whisk me back to my lovely home.

By the time the bus showed up I'd come down from my high and my phone was telling me it was 5:30. This wouldn't be the first time this has happened to me, and it of course would not be the last. I would've taken a taxi home, but I'd spent all my money on McDonalds, so I was shit out of luck. I got home around 6:30, went to my bed, and slept until

6:30 at night. I called the bros after that and asked what they did, and they said they'd gone to White Castle and then hung out in Derek's attic and answered questions for an interview they were doing with a music blog. Apparently Sos answered "No" to every question, due to not giving a damn because he felt so awful. I was so jealous, White Castle would've been perfect after that night.

HALLOWEEN

One holiday I never got to really enjoy had to have been Halloween. Growing up I was constantly moving back and forth from place to place, so I never had a solid group of friends with which to go out and celebrate with, but this year would prove to be different. I had The Collective We to hang out with! Ramy was planning a big backyard party at his house that would be loaded with food, bands, decorations, the whole nine. He really went all out for it, to the point where he had me ride with him to Party City several times during the time leading up to the party to get shit.

That year Halloween was set for a Friday, so to make it a whole day affair that everyone could come to he set the party up for the next day. This suddenly went from a Halloween party to a Halloween weekend, so I figured why not make plans for Friday night too? I went all out this year, I ordered myself a brand new black and white Adidas tracksuit and a dreadlock wig so I could go as Jonathan Davis from Korn, a dare set out to me by Alex weeks before. I say dare because he makes these suggestions as a joke thinking I won't actually do it, well joke's on him.

The day before Halloween my wig and tracksuit came in the mail and I decided I wanted to go into the city to celebrate. I made plans to hang out with Derek, as he lived in the city and definitely didn't have any prior engagements. I got on the 190 bus from Rutherford to New York, popped on my iPod, and got myself in the mood to cruise for ladies.

While riding the bus I got a text message from Tom's friend, the one who held the after-party for Alex and the Horribles. He invited me to come over for a Halloween party he was throwing, this was finally my chance to find Dani and talk to her again! Not only that, but now we had a plan for the evening instead of just walking around town without anywhere to be. I got to Derek's place and I asked him if he wanted to go, and he was down, but first we needed good eats.

Not only did we need good eats, but Derek didn't have a costume. So we went to KFC and I loaded my gullet with chicken while Derek had mac n' cheese and mashed potatoes (due to him being a vegetarian at the time). If you've never experienced a New York City Halloween, let me spin it for you quick. Everyone's in costume. Everyone. You see Lady Gaga in those ridiculous outfits at her concerts, that's what everyone in New York looks like on Halloween. Even in the local KFC, which was packed with people from wall to wall.

What happened at this KFC that night was something special. While we were eating our meals, the doors opened and everyone went quiet. In walked the most perfect Colonel Sanders, who walked right up to the counter and ordered a bucket of "Kentucky's finest." The cashier handed him his order, and he turned to everyone and said "I traveled a LONG way for this!" and the store erupted in laughter and applause. It was so perfect, and you can tell it wasn't planned by the restaurant because all the employees were just as surprised as we were. He walked out with his bucket of glory and went off to whatever party he himself was invited to.

After we finished our chicken we showed ourselves to the door and headed down the block to the specialty store that popped up every year that sold Halloween costumes and decorations. I forget what Derek was looking for, I don't think he even knew what he wanted. I think he was looking for a mustache, but couldn't find one. They wound up having more product than we thought, but it was still too little too late as they didn't have anything he wanted. Or maybe he was just picky. Either way, we wound up back at his dorm where he decided he was going to go as a summer tourist. He put on a silly straw hat, tie-die shirt with a camera around his neck, and the silliest little boy swim trunks he had. And he had quite a few pairs, I might add. While he was getting changed I explained to him how awesome it was going to be to go to that party and run into Dani by chance (planned chance) and finally get her number. Maybe we'd go out on a date, and she'd fall in love with me as we walked hand in hand down St. Mark's Place. Maybe she'd rest her head on my shoulder, with her arm around mine.

"Dude, Derek, she's the PERFECT girl!" I said to him excitedly.

"Kail you literally tell me every girl you see is the 'perfect' girl. Every time you think you have a chance with a girl you say she's perfect, then you wind up hating her when she rejects you!"

"Yeah but Derek you don't understand, she's PERFECT for me! We're gonna go out and fall in love and everything will be perfect and she'll hang out with our crew and one day we'll move in together and everything will be awesome."

"If you say so, man." By this point he had given up on trying to explain to me that I get too attached too quickly. At the time I would see a girl and instead of just talking to her like a person I would assume she was the second coming of Christ and get too excited about what could happen. Basically I was a hopeless romantic.

We're about to go when I decided I had to take a leak, so I went to the bathroom. As I'm draining the main vein, there's a knock at the door and I hear a girl's voice talking.

"Hey, is Cho here?" The girl asks Derek, who tells her he hasn't been home all day.

You see, Derek had this crazy Asian roommate that always gave us the creeps. I forget his real name, and I don't want him to sue me, so I'll just call him Cho. We gave him the nickname because this was right after the Virginia Tech massacre had gone down, and this kid looked and acted exactly like Seung-Hui Cho.

Anyways, I hear this girl outside the bathroom asking for him and I open the door to the bathroom before I could get the chance to wash my hands and I go "Gurlz?!"

It was actually two really cute girls, one Middle Eastern, the other Asian. They had been friends of Cho's and had made plans to hang out with him for Halloween. Since Cho wasn't in at the moment, me and Derek both started working our charms on them. He was talking to the little Asian chick and I was talking to the Middle East Mama.

"So Cho actually talks to you guys?" I asked her as a way to break the ice. It wasn't just a really bad ice breaker, I was genuinely interested.

"Yeah, he doesn't talk much, but we're pretty good friends. So do you go to this school?"

"No, I'm just here hanging out with my friend Derek, we were gonna go to a party tonight."

"Wait so you're straight? Oh, that is such a relief! Every guy at this school is gay, so it's tough as shit to get cock." She then sunk into one of the chairs.

"Yeah I'm straight AND single." I was hoping she wanted my peepee in her mouth.

We talked for the better part of a half hour and every so often I'd look over at Derek and see him talking to the Asian girl. These girls were totally into us and were willing to mess around, but I had my sights set on Dani. And to add to it, I could tell they were a little buzzed from pre-gaming and the last thing I wanna do is get with a chick who ain't all the way there. I'd been trying to signal to Derek that we should split before things got a little silly, but he wasn't paying attention. Eventually Cho walked in the door and for the first time I was delighted to see him. It wasn't that I wasn't interested in the Middle Eastern chick, it was just that she had a few to drink and I didn't, and she wasn't Dani. I had goals for that night, dammit, and I needed to see them through.

After Cho walked in the door the girls practically forgot about us, so me and Derek booked it out the door. We were an hour late for the party and I wasn't going to miss on my one chance to land this chick. I'd been given a redo, an extra life, a mulligan, and I wasn't about to waste it. So we hopped on the train to Brooklyn and what seemed to be certain victory. We'd gotten there maybe around 9 o'clock, and as we were walking down the street towards Tom's friend's place we ran into one of Tom's roommates and his lady friend. They recognized us, said hi, and asked if we were going to the party. I jokingly told them that we were "excited for the gurlz," and the lady friend didn't get the joke. I later found out she thought I was mentally handicapped, not even like she said "is that kid retarded?" She legitimately thought I was autistic, and because of that I hated her for the longest time. Truth be told, I never saw her again after that night, so it didn't really matter anyways.

We got to the party and walked in and immediately Tom's friend gave us hugs and showed us around. Knowing my tastes, he made sure there was more than enough gurlz and lunch, but couldn't help me out with the money. I was delighted at the food he had laid out, and the gurlz were, of course, top notch. He didn't stick around much, because he was the host and had other guests to see himself to. So I looked around, but couldn't find Dani anywhere. I introduced myself to some people, had some small talk, but I was really disappointed that Dani wasn't there. The host was chilling on the roof with another group, so me and Derek went up there to investigate.

"Hey, dude, is Dani coming tonight?" I asked him.

"Dani? Dani who?"

"The chick I was talking to at the last party, short black hair, a little thick, red lipstick."

"Sorry, dude, I'm drawin' a blank. I barely even remember the last party."

"Ah, dammit!"

Discouraged, me and Derek went back downstairs and he said he wasn't really feeling the party. There was no one there we knew, the one dude we knew was busy with other people, and the whole reason we went there decided not to show up. The night was pretty much over anyways, so fuck it. We made our way out the door and started heading back. As we got out the door, though, there was this homeless girl sitting on a blanket on the sidewalk. She asked if I had any change, and I looked at her and I said "you know what, here's a twenty" and I gave her a $20 bill. We'd later become good friends, but that's another story for another day. She was so grateful, she wished us a Happy Halloween and we were on our way.

Disappointed with not being able to score that night, I looked at Derek and I said "You know, the night's still young, maybe there's chance for me to score yet."

"What do you mean?"

"Watch this." I said to him with a smug, confident look in my eyes.

I motioned over to the other side of the train, there were two girls sitting there. One dressed as a witch, the other dressed as Freddy Krueger. I went to the Freddy Krueger one and I started talking to her, it was like I wasn't the same ol' shy Kris Kail who talks about gurlz, but doesn't actually go for them. I told her I thought she made a very good Freddy Krueger, and that she had an adorable costume. She said thanks, and then proceeded to ignore me.

Ouch.

Luckily our stop was next, I've never gotten shot down harder in my whole life. It was pretty awful. Especially because I lied about that being our stop, that was Derek's stop, I was going to ride the train to Times Square so I could hop on the bus and head home. So I wound up getting off at that stop to avoid the embarrassment, and then I walked with Derek to his dorm and hung out for a few before splitting. It was a disappointing night, but tomorrow was another day.

My sweet ass Jonathan Davis costume, notice how I'm not wearing the dreadlock wig I bought.

RAMY'S PARTY

Going home that night was disappointing, as I walked away without succeeding where I have failed so many times, but there was still hope yet. The next day was Ramy's big Halloween party, the one I'd helped him buy decorations for. I'd planned on this being the fall back plan, because I knew I'd know basically every girl there. When you're not exactly the best looking guy, and on top of that you're also not the most suave guy, getting with girls who know you already can be a little tricky. To be honest, I couldn't land a date throughout high school with anyone from Rutherford High School. Who wants to date the class clown? In high school relationships are all about status, and you don't gain much status by dating Kris Kail.

Knowing Ramy, his guest list would consist mostly of kids from our high school, but at the same time he had outside friends he could invite. This lead to Ramy's party being the backup, the chances of me scoring were slim, but there was still a very small chance. Also, Ramy was one of the good kids in high school, i.e. he didn't drink. I was the same way, but really getting with chicks was pretty difficult when there wasn't alcohol present. Closing the deal with a sober girl wouldn't become a master skill of mine until I'd already moved out of my parent's house, so of course I would have some difficulty here.

The party started around seven o'clock and because Ramy had worked so hard and spent a ton of money to make the party awesome, there was a five dollar cover to get in. Normally I hate covers to parties, but because Ramy put so much work into it I didn't mind pretending to help during the day so I didn't have to pay the five dollars to get in. I really don't remember doing much, I think I hid in his childhood tree house for most of the day. I'm such a good friend, I cheated my bro out of five dollars and didn't even help him set up.

Tons of people came, and nearly everyone was in costume. A lot of people showed up, but immediately turned around when they found out there wasn't going to be any alcohol. It was a bummer, but really there was more than enough people anyways and the people that were there were really fun to hang around with. One thing that kind of bothered me was how everyone I knew from high school would ask me what I was doing with myself, seeing as I'd just graduated high school the June before, and my only answer was "working at Blockbuster." That was kind of embarrassing for me, I was always kind of ashamed at how I didn't go to college, so I was never the kind to return to my high school after I graduated. I went to a play or two here and there, but really I tried to stay far away.

As I had assumed, I knew everybody that came to the party. They were all mostly high school juniors and seniors. They were younger than me seeing how at this point I would've been a college freshman. It was disappointing, but I still had fun. At one point this chick walked in dressed as Sarah Palin, an extremely hot Sarah Palin. Not knowing anyone that would look like that, I figured this was one of Ramy's friends that I didn't know, so I went to hit on her. As I got close, I realized it was this kid Patrick, who I knew, and who wasn't a female at all. Sometimes I wondered if he was even male, but I try not to think too hard about that. He was a fun kid, but not my type. I prefer fat chicks and lusty toilets, for those who don't remember or didn't read the first book.

Later into the night a group of stoner kids showed up, two girls and a dude. The dude I'd known since freshman year, he was this awesome hippie dude who kind of looked like Josh from Drake and Josh, that's what I'll call him. Josh was accompanied by two lovely ladies: a short, somewhat plump young thang I'll call Amanda, and another, slimmer gal I'll refer to as Miranda. Throughout senior year I had a huge crush on Amanda, and her friend Miranda had a pretty sizable crush on me, though I didn't really know her because she didn't go to our school.

They came and checked out the very end of the party, but weren't really interested seeing as nobody had pot or beer. They invited me and Sos to come over Amanda's house to smoke in her basement. Sos wasn't exactly interested, but I needed a wingman so I begged him to come with. He eventually caved and he drove us to her house, which was on the other side of town. We'd shown up fashionably late to her after party, which consisted of her, Josh, and Miranda, and they were fresh out of pot. There was like one last toke on their blunt left, so I inhaled with all of my might. Knowing I needed the beeriest of muscles, I grabbed the bottle of vodka they'd been sharing and chugged the whole thing down. I was destined to score, no matter what the cost.

The next morning I woke up naked in my bed, all the lights were on, the TV was off (I normally sleep with it on), and I had no idea where my glasses and cell phone were. I freaked the fuck out. How the Hell did I wind up naked in my own bed without my glasses or cell phone? For reference, if I take off my glasses I'm immediately blind. I couldn't tell you how many fingers you were holding up if they were right in my face. The worst part of this was the fact that it was 11:30 AM and I had to be at work at 12:00 PM. I was boned.

I ran over to my computer to see if anyone was on AIM who could give me a ride and help me find my glasses and cell phone. Maybe along the way I could remember what the Hell had happened the night before, but that wasn't important. What was important was that I got my stuff back.

Lucky for me, Nick Dubs was on AIM, so I IMed him and told him what happened and begged him to give me a lift. He knew I was in danger, so he said "fuck it, here goes my Sunday" and he came to my rescue. While he was on his way, Josh and Amanda both commented on my Facebook telling me each had a respective article of mine. Josh had my cell phone, and he lived right around the corner from me, so when Nick got to my place we made that our first destination.

We got to his house and Josh came out with my phone in hand, it had tons of scratches on it, but I didn't care.

"Yeah, this was in the backseat of my car. You were pretty fucked up, dude." He said as he handed it to me.

"Thanks, dude, I gotta get to Amanda's house so she can give me my glasses. Fill me in on what happened last night another time."

"Dude, you'd have to take a whole day off from work to hear this story. It's a classic, classic Kail." He laughed, obviously something funny had happened the night before. I didn't care, I just wanted to get to work.

I called Amanda and she said Miranda would take my glasses out to the car when we got there. We pulled up to her house and Miranda was waiting outside, she walked over and handed me the glasses and stormed off. It was obvious she wasn't at all pleased to see me, which was a signal for alarm because normally she loved me. Oh well, didn't matter. I had five minutes to get to Blockbuster.

Dubs dropped me off outside the store and I slapped him some skin and told him I totally owed him one. He told me to find out what the fuck I'd done the night before and then fill him in and we'd be even. I laughed and agreed, and then I headed into the store.

I got into the store and my manager Mike told me I was an hour early. Really? I went through all that just to be an hour early? He said it was okay and told me just to go clock in, so that's what I did. In all the excitement, I hadn't even noticed I was feeling like shit, so before I went to the back I went to the bathroom. What started off as me trying to shake a headache became me vomiting violently in the toilet. Good grief.

This repeated itself for the next hour and a half, and finally Mike realized I wasn't feeling so good, so he told me to go home. It was Sunday, nobody rents movies on Sundays, so he sent me home. I called

Sos and asked him if he could pick me up, and five minutes later he was outside the store.

"Dude, you came into work hung over?" He asked as I got in his car.

"Well, I didn't realize I was hung over. I woke up naked in my bed without any blankets, the lights were all on, and I didn't have my glasses or cell phone. I was so confused over that that I realize I was hung over."

"Not surprised, the way you acted last night. That was the funniest thing in the world. You're the worst drunk ever."

"What do you mean?"

"You don't remember anything?"

"No, I remember grabbing the bottle of vodka, and the next minute I was naked in bed."

"You don't remember 'Duuuudeee, gurlz?'"

"What?"

"You kept saying 'Dude, Gurlz!' the whole night! Along with a slew of other catch phrases. It was hysterical."

Sos filled me in on what happened. Apparently, after I started drinking the vodka I became really nutty and I was seriously hitting on Amanda. She wasn't exactly interested, so she tried to dump me on Miranda, who had been looking to hook up with someone (specifically me), and I annoyed the piss out of Miranda. Eventually, Miranda set her sights on Sos, who didn't smell like Robert Downey Jr. in the 90's. He was there pretty much just to baby sit me, but Amanda decided to hook him up with Miranda.

Miranda took Sos to another part of the basement that was curtained off, and I kept wanting to know what the heck they were up to. The whole time I kept pulling the curtain aside and peaking over and going "dudeeeee, gurlzzzz" to Sos, which I guess meant that I was signaling to him that there was, in fact, a female present and that he should attempt to succeed. Hoping to let her friend get some in peace, Amanda got Josh to take me outside where we'd go for a walk and let off some steam. I was apparently running around shouting random Dragon Ball Z quotes the whole time, yelling out things like "I will make this whole planet suffer!" and "Me turn you to chocolate!" and "I ain't goin' back to jail." That last one wasn't Dragon Ball Z, but for some reason I kept sayin' it.

Josh remembered his little brother had made pot brownies earlier that day, so he decided to go get some. We piled into his car and I was sitting in the back trying to Kamehameha Josh the whole time. I didn't realize that by doing that I'd kill us all, luckily I don't have Super Saiyan powers. We got to his house and he handed Amanda the brownies and she made me hold them.

"Me love chocolate" I said as I inhaled a good three or four brownies.

They immediately began yelling at me. Of course, who was I to know each of those brownies went for $10 on the streets? How silly of them to entrust someone who was already drunk off of two-thirds of a bottle of vodka with a plate of pot brownies. I then passed out in the back seat and we went back to Amanda's house, where they dragged me back into the basement and laid me out on the floor. Miranda took one look at me as they laid me out, and I began projectile vomiting all over the place. Sos had fallen asleep, and I was knocked out cold laying in a pool of my own vomit, so they decided the right thing to do would be to let me sleep in it and not wake up Sos.

Around three or four in the morning, Sos woke up and realized he wasn't in his own bed. He looked over and saw me lying shirtless in a puddle of my own vomit, and realized what had happened. He picked me up and put my arm around his shoulder so he could carry me to the car. After tossing me in the passenger's side, he got in and drove me home. As we're driving, he hears me making vomit-noises and starts yelling at me to do it out the window as he rolls it down for me. I dry heave out the window a little, and then I began shouting random numbers at Sos. These numbers sounded non-sensical, but Sos eventually realized that they were the combo to the back door of the house.

He walked me up to the back door and opened it and pushed me in and told me to find my own damn way up to my bed room. He also told me to eat some bread, and that it would soak up the alcohol in my

Not a picture from that night specifically, but this is how I looked when I was a stinkin' drunk teen.

stomach. I told him I'd eat a whole loaf, and then as soon as he left I made my way up the stairs and right to my bed. I'd turned the light on and not even bothered turning the TV on, and I got undressed so I wouldn't wear gross vomit clothes in my sleep. I then passed out on my bed, where I would wake up a few hours later in a complete daze.

We arrived outside my house by the time Sos had finished filling me in on what happened the night before, and it all started to make sense. Amanda had Miranda bring out my glasses because she was busy cleaning up my vomit, and Miranda was pissed likely because the whole night was spent looking after a drunken moron.

I got out of the car, told Sos I'd owed him one, slapped him some of the proverbial skin, and went inside. I immediately took some medicine and got into bed and slept the rest of the day away.

So in conclusion, Halloween turned out to be a bust, but like the Titanic, it was the most glorious failure I'd ever experienced. I'd failed at getting laid many times, but this was by far the most exciting time I'd ever lost out on the chance to even smell a girl's puss. I learned a lot that weekend about my friends and about myself. Since that weekend I've refused to ever drink vodka again, and it wouldn't be much longer before I gave up drinking completely.

EPILOGUE

214

Putting this book together has been a trip down memory lane for me. Research for it mainly consisted of sitting at Taco Bell with my friends shooting the shit and talking about old times. Something my father always told me was that when you're old as shit the one thing you have left is stories. At the end of the day all we have are our memories, be them happy memories or sad memories. Most of the things my dad has said to me in my life have gone in one ear and right out the other because he doesn't know shit about what the fuck he's talking about, but that always stuck with me. Being able to sit at Taco Bell with all my friends from high school and talk about all the shit we used to do as kids is probably the best thing in the world to me right now.

The sad thing about all that is that I'm only twenty-one. I skipped college and went straight into working a full-time job, and when you do that you lose out on the opportunity to hang out with people your own age. Most of the people I see now are ten to fifteen years older than me, and I don't mind that at all. The guys I work with are some of the best people to hang around with. My old friends from my days in the Collective We are all busy with their own lives – playing in bands, working, finishing up college, girlfriends. It's hard to get together with them, even though me, Alex, and Nick Dubs try to get together every now and then.

The reason why I think that's sad is because I let go of my youth at an early age to make way for a life as a responsible adult, so I can't go out and make more juvenile stories like I used to. Working a full-time job and taking care of a pregnant girlfriend while making way for a new-born baby boy due in the summer has really made me stop and think about life. I'm mature and responsible enough to be able to handle the life that's right around the corner, but sometimes I get nostalgic about the old days and worry that they're gone forever. I've been stone cold sober since July 2011, right after my twenty-first birthday, so there aren't going to be any more drunken Kail stories. I'm in a steady relationship with a woman I love and want to be with, so how are there supposed to be goofy dating stories if I'm not dating? I've been going over these in my head for the past few weeks, worried that the rest of my life is going to be monotonous at best.

The truth is, I don't know what's going to happen from here on out. I don't know if I'll become the most famous dude who ever lived, or if I'll be a standard dad who does his job and takes care of his kids, or if I'll find a way to juggle my home, my job, and my friends successfully. Chances are I have nothing to worry about though, because it's not like my friends aren't going through the same or similar things.

Alex, for instance, is finishing up college right now while playing guitar and singing in the band Harpoon Forever. He works at his college's radio station as a DJ, and he's interned at the world famous WFMU in Jersey City, NJ where he writes for their website which has been named one of Time's 100 best blogs. Nick Dubs works for a car dealership doing God knows what while he's finishing up college too. He makes a ton of money and totally paid for pizza for us once. I should hang out with him more often. Derek graduated college last year and works as an actor now, he usually does bit roles in commercials, but has appeared in music videos (such as the Solja Boy Tell 'Em/Andrew W.K./Matt and Kim collaboration I'm a Goner) and he performs on stage as well. Sos graduated last year and he's delivering pizzas and working out at the gym a lot while he takes classes working towards getting his masters. Ramy is a stand-up comedian who's constantly between NYC and L.A. doing his thing, while Catman is MIA (he stopped talking to us once he went to college). Teller works full time right now and is always busy between his job and girlfriend, we haven't talked much since we stopped doing Destroy All Slackers, but that's neither of our faults. Pete works full time as an engineer for a New York City firm, I think, I really don't know what he does. All I know is he makes a lot more money than I do. Everyone else? They're busy with whatever. Point is, we're all busy now that high school's over.

And you know what? I'm okay with all of that. I'm fine with my life the way it is. If I never reach super-stardom, I'll at least be happy knowing that there is a small, but loyal following of slackers who love reading the stories I have to tell. And that, my friends, is The Prestige. The fact that you actually paid good money for this book is what's extraordinary, and the fact that I was able to keep you reading until this point is me taking the extraordinary and turning it on its head.

I've been thinking that this might be the last book I write about my crazy life, but I have a few more stories that I might want to tell down the line. Not only that, but I do have a kid on the way, so chances are there'll be some mighty interesting stories there. One thing I know for sure is that I will never stop writing. As long as you people like what I have to say, I'll continue to write about my stories and thoughts on pop culture.

My favorite movie as a kid was Don Bluth's All Dogs Go to Heaven. It's about a dog getting his ass killed by another dog because he was competition in the gambling business of the 1930's New Orleans underworld. Thinking about it, the plot doesn't make sense, but there was one song in the movie called You Can't Keep a Good Dog Down. And there's some truth to that statement. That phrase has stayed with me my whole life, and now I can pass it on to you guys. No matter what I face in my life, I know I'll come out swingin'. You can't keep a good slacker down!

ABOUT THE AUTHOR

Kris Kail is a comedian from New Jersey who's been active since 2006. After performing at numerous open mic nights with friend Derek Spaldo, Kail went solo and recorded four successful comedy albums – *Fun and Fancy Free*, *Kail Legends*, *Humor Songs*, and *Devil May Kail*. He also co-hosted the highly successful comedy podcast *Destroy All Slackers* with friend Andrew Teller.

Kail currently runs the comedy website *Kail's Big Time Burger Joint*, as well as having written for Kotaku. Kail's been mentioned and ripped apart by numerous high profile blogs for his antics such as The Verge, ScrewAttack, TSSZ News, and GoNintendo. In 2010 he released his first book *Slacker's Paradise – The Collective Writings of an Internet Radio Host*, which has gone on to achieve cult status. Kail currently lives in Hackensack, NJ with his girlfriend Katie and cat Mookie. He's expecting his first child in the Summer of 2012.

You can find Kail online at:
http://www.dudegurlz.com/
http://www.twitter.com/DudeGurlz

ACKNOWLEDGEMENTS

There are tons of people I'd like to thank for making this book possible. I'd like to thank my mom and dad for having unprotected sex one night, my brother for teaching me how to be awesome, my sister and her awesome kids for existing I guess, the rest of my family for saying nice things because they have to, my darling girlfriend Katie for always being super supportive of me even when I give her a rude 'tude, our cat Mookie for being super cute and super sweet, my unborn child which the doctor says is a boy, but could possibly be a girl, Fred "Trunks" Wood for being one of the closest friends I have in "the biz" and for offering to write the foreword for this book, Dazz and Charlie for being cool cats, all the guys at work who jokingly made fun of me but secretly knew I was awesome (I hope you guys weren't actually making fun of me), the Blockbuster crew of Jay-Rey, Joe Naz, Lori, CR, Dreena, Keith, and Lauren for putting up with my antics, the Collective We: Alex Goldstein, Nick Dubs, Tom Malach, Derek Spaldo, Ramy Youssef, Sos, Chris Romaglia, Vin Landolfi, Jay Patel, Andrew Teller, Pete Manse, Paul Gormley, Chris Catoya, Cesar Arakaki, and Danny Arakaki for always being there for me and always giving me great stories to tell later on, Tinky, Moony, and Kit-Kat for being the Kail Gurlz, all listeners of Destroy All Slackers who constantly e-mail me and tweet me asking when we're gonna record new episodes, the Twitter crew: PTCruiserUSA, SPAGETTABOUTIT, CrooklynHuffer, tunam3lt, jessenicho, namodyn, DanMoffTarkin, Aangot, Dinophobia, hammerofchrist, DrewPickles, ShadowDude112, SerenaMidori, IAmArique, shutupno1cares, tinaodarby, rwoodsmall, CMezmerize, imabeagle, ButtJensen, ioneknewa, smartfelly, namcospeedway, helloiamarfy, n00neimp0rtant, megadrivesonic, Skittle61, danieleastman, varylarge, pop_champagne, lulinternet, MyCatEdwin, jova7587, sad_tire, sonichu1, NekoAleu, JonnyWags, HelloClaireese, SwagCracker, thebigchonus, Tree_Bag, honky_dory, catpizzas, Cool_Toes, mattytalks, arrest_that_ass, hamsandcastle, danxdeathcore, DankDevice, rad_milk, anarchistcorgi, and beebee880, and to everyone else! Also, to all the people out there that honestly believe my stuff is worth reading, thanks so much! You guys rule!

COPYRIGHT

www.ingramcontent.com/pod-product-compliance
Lightning Source LLC
Chambersburg PA
CBHW071957040426
42447CB00009B/1372